Welcome to Table Talk

Table Talk helps children and adults explore the Bible together. Each day provides a short family Bible time which, with your own adaptation, could work for ages 4 to 12. It includes optional follow-on material which takes the passage further for older children. There are also suggestions for linking **Table Talk** with **XTB** children's notes.

Who can use Table Talk?

- **Families**
- **One adult with one child**
- **A teenager with a younger brother or sister**
- **Children's leaders with their groups**
- **Any other mix that works for you!**

Table Talk
A short family Bible time for daily use. Table Talk takes about five minutes, maybe at breakfast, or after an evening meal. Choose whatever time and place suits you best as a family. Table Talk includes a simple discussion starter or activity that leads into a short Bible reading. This is followed by a few questions.

XTB
XTB children's notes help 7-11 year olds to get into the Bible for themselves. They are based on the same Bible passages as **Table Talk**. You will find suggestions for how **XTB** can be used alongside **Table Talk** on the next page.

In the next three pages you'll find suggestions for how to use Table Talk, along with hints and tips for adapting it to your own situation. If you've never done anything like this before, check out our web page for further help (go to www.thegoodbook.co.uk and click on Daily Reading) or write in for a fact sheet.

THE SMALL PRINT

Table Talk is published by The Good Book Company, 37 Elm Road, New Malden, Surrey, KT3 3HB
Tel: 0845 225 0880. www.thegoodbook.co.uk   email: Alison@thegoodbook.co.uk   Written by Alison Mitchell and Mark Tomlinson. Fab pictures by Kirsty McAllister. Bible quotations taken from the Good News Bible.
AUSTRALIA: Distributed by Matthias Media. Tel: (02) 9663 1478; email: info@matthiasmedia.com.au

HOW TO USE Table Talk

Table Talk is designed to last for up to three month How you use it depends on what works for you. V have included 65 full days of material in this issue plus some more low-key suggestions for another 2 days (at the back of the book). We would like to encourage you to work at establishing a pattern o family reading. The first two weeks are the hardes

KEYPOINT
This is the main point you should be trying to convey. Don't read this out—it often gives away the end of the story!

Table Talk is based on the same Bible passages as *XTB*, but usually only asks for two or three verses to be read out loud. The full *XTB* passage is listed at the top of each Table Talk page. If you are using Table Talk with older children, read the full *XTB* passage rather than the shorter version.

The main part of Table Talk is designed to be suitable for younger children. *Building Up* includes more difficult questions designed for older children, or those with more Bible knowledge.

As far as possible, if your children are old enough to read the Bible verses for themselves, encourage them to find the answers in the passage and to tell you which verse the answer is in. This will help them to get used to handling the Bible for themselves.

The *Building Up* section is optional. It is designed to build on the passage studied in Table Talk (and XTB). Building Up includes some additional questions which reinforce the main teaching point, apply the teaching more directly, or follow up any difficult issues raised by the passage.

Linking with *XTB*

The **XTB** children's notes are based on the same passages as **Table Talk**. There are a number of ways in which you can link the two together:
• Children do **XTB** on their own. Parents then follow these up later (see suggestions below).
• A child and adult work through **XTB** together.
• A family uses **Table Talk** together at breakfast. Older children then use **XTB** on their own later.
• You use **Table Talk** on its own, with no link to **XTB**.

FOLLOWING UP XTB

If your child uses **XTB** on their own it can be helpful to ask them later to show you (or tell you) what they've done. Some useful starter questions are:

• Can you tell me what the reading was about?

• Is there anything you didn't understand or want to ask about?

• Did anything surprise you in the reading? Was there anything that would have surprised the people who first saw it or read about it?

• What did you learn about God, Jesus or the Holy Spirit?

• Is there anything you're going to do as a result of reading this passage?

Table Talk is deliberately not too ambitious. Most families find it quite hard to set up a regular pattern of reading the Bible together—and when they do meet, time is often short. So **Table Talk** is designed to be quick and easy to use, needing little in the way of extra materials, apart from pen and paper now and then.

BUT!!

Most families have special times when they **can** be more ambitious, or do have some extra time available. Here are some suggestions for how you can use **Table Talk** as the basis for a special family adventure...

Have an adventure!

FOOD!
Eat some food linked with the passage you are studying. For example Manna (biscuits made with honey, Exodus 16v31), Unleavened bread or Honeycomb (Matthew 3v4—but don't try the locusts!)

DISPLAY AREA
We find it easier to remember and understand what we learn when we have something to look at. Make a Table Talk display area, for pictures, Bible verses and prayers. Add to it regularly.

VIDEO
A wide range of Bible videos are available—from simple cartoon stories, to whole Gospels filmed with real life actors. (Your local Christian bookshop should have a range.) Choose one that ties in with the passages you are reading together. **Note:** Use the video **in addition** to the Bible passage, not **instead** of it!

PICNIC
Take Table Talk with you on a family picnic. Thank God for His beautiful Creation.

WALK
Go for a walk together. Stop somewhere with a good view and read Genesis 1v1—2v4.

GETTING TOGETHER
Invite another family for a meal, and to read the Bible together. The children could make a poster based on the passage.

MUSEUM
Visit a museum to see a display from Bible times. Use it to remind yourselves that the Bible tells us about real people and real history.

PRAYER DIARY
As a special project, make a family prayer diary. Use it to keep a note of things you pray for—and the answers God gives you. This can be a tremendous help to children (and parents!) to learn to trust God in prayer as we see how He answers over time.

Go on—try it!

HOLIDAYS
Set aside a special time each day while on holiday. Choose some unusual places to read the Bible together—on the beach, up a mountain, in a boat... Take some photos to put on your Table Talk display when you get back from holiday.

You could try one of the special holiday editions of XTB and Table Talk—**Christmas Unpacked**, **Easter Unscrambled** and **Summer Signposts**.

DRAMA OR PUPPETS
Take time to dramatise a Bible story. Maybe act it out (with costumes if possible) or make some simple puppets to retell the story.

Enough of the introduction, let's get going...

DAYS 1-20
Notes for Parents

MARK'S GOSPEL
Gospel means "good news". Mark's book tells us the good news about Jesus. It's divided into two halves...

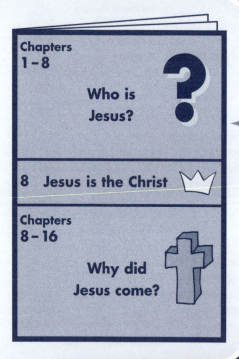

EVIDENCE CHART
If you used Issue Five of Table Talk (The Promise Keeper) you may still have a copy of this chart. It shows evidence from Mark chapters 1 and 2 that Jesus has the same <u>authority</u> as God.

EVIDENCE CHART

Jesus is in charge—He has the same authority as God

- Authority over **people**. (Mark 1v20)
- Authority as a **teacher**. (Mark 1v22)
- Authority over **evil spirits**. (Mark 1v26)
- Authority over **sickness**. (Mark 1v31)
- Authority to **forgive sins**. (Mark 2v10)

DAY 1
Who is this?

KEYPOINT
Even the wind and the waves obey **Jesus**—because He is the Son of God.

Today's passages are:
Table Talk: Mark 4v35-41
XTB: Mark 4v35-41

 TABLE TALK
Find a sheet (blue if you have one) and spread it on the floor (as Lake Galilee). Sit round it for today's Table Talk.

We're reading Mark's book about Jesus. Look at the diagram in Notes for Parents to see how Mark divided his book into two halves. In this issue of Table Talk we're reading chapters 4 to 8, so we'll be finding out more about **who** Jesus is.

 READ
Read the story from Mark 4. As the storm grows, start to *flap the sheet* to make the waves. Keep flapping until Jesus <u>stops</u> the storm. **Read Mark 4v35-41**

 TALK
Where was Jesus when the storm started? (v38) (*Asleep, at the back of the boat.*) The storm didn't wake Jesus! What did? (38) (*The terrified disciples, who rudely accused Him of not caring about them!*) What happened when Jesus spoke to the storm? (v39) (*The wind died down and the sea was calm.*) How did the disciples feel now? (v41) (*Terrified!*)

 THINK
Read the disciples question again (v41). How would <u>you</u> answer it? (*The wind and waves obey Jesus, because He is the Son of God. He's in charge of nature—has authority over it.*)

 PRAY
Ask God to help you to learn more about His Son Jesus as you read Mark's book.

Building up
In the first half of Mark's book we see Jesus' amazing authority. Look at the list in **Notes for Parents**. Today's miracle adds to that list (showing authority over <u>nature</u>).

DAY 2
Demon destroyer

KEYPOINT
Jesus has authority over evil spirits. He is <u>far</u> more powerful than they are!

Today's passages are:
Table Talk: Mark 5v6-13
XTB: Mark 5v1-13

 TABLE TALK

Yesterday we read about Jesus calming a **violent storm**. Why was He able to do that? (He's the Son of God, with the same authority as God.) Today, Jesus meets a **violent man**. Jesus calms him, too.

 READ

This man had an evil spirit living in him. It made him violent. Nobody could help him, so he lived alone among the tombs in the hills. *With older children, read the whole passage—***Mark 5v1-13**. *With younger children, read* **Mark 5v6-13**.

 TALK

The evil spirits knew who Jesus was. What did they call Him? (v7) (*Son of the Most High God.*)

Sometimes in the Bible we read about evil spirits. They are God's enemies, and often made people ill. But look back at the list of Jesus' authority on Day 1. What does it tell you about evil spirits? (*That Jesus has authority over them—He's in charge.*)

The evil spirits <u>knew</u> Jesus was in charge. Where did they beg Him to let them go? (v12) (*Into the pigs.*) Jesus let them—and the whole herd rushed into the water.

Sometime, reading about evil spirits can be scary. But Jesus is far more powerful than any evil spirit! So we don't need to be afraid. Thank God that Jesus has power over evil.

PRAY

Building up
Look back to Mark's first account of Jesus driving out an evil spirit in **Mark 1v23-27**. Here too, the evil spirit <u>had</u> to obey Jesus. Jesus is **in charge!** (*If they're worried, reassure your child that there's nothing to worry about. They cannot be "possessed" if Jesus is their King. He is far more powerful than the power of evil.*)

DAY 3
Spot the difference

KEYPOINT
Jesus made a huge difference to the man who had been freed from evil spirits.

Today's passages are:
Table Talk: Mark 5v14-20
XTB: Mark 5v14-20

 TABLE TALK

<u>Spot the Difference:</u> Send one person out of the room. Make a change in your appearance (e.g. undo a button, take off a hair ribbon). Call the first person back and see if they can spot the difference.

 READ

Jesus made a HUGE difference to the man who'd had evil spirits in him. **Before**, he was violent, kept breaking his chains, and had to live alone among the tombs. **Afterwards**, he was very different... **Read Mark 5v14-20**

 TALK

What was the man like now? (v15) (*Sitting quietly, dressed properly and in his right man.*) You'd expect the local people to be pleased for the man, but how did they actually feel? (v15) (*Afraid*) What did they want Jesus to do? (v17) (*Leave!*) The healed man wanted to go with Jesus, but what did Jesus tell him to do instead? (v19) (*Go home to his family—he probably hadn't seen them for a long time!—and tell them what Jesus had done.*) Did the man just tell his family? (v20) (*No, he went round the ten towns known as the Decapolis, telling everyone!*)

If you're Christians, then Jesus has done **great things** for you, too. Ask God to help you to tell someone about Jesus this week.

PRAY

Building up
<u>Spot the Difference:</u> Read **v17-18** again. What's the difference between the two reactions to Jesus? Pray for someone you know who <u>doesn't</u> know Jesus. Pray that they won't turn their back on Jesus (like the local people did) but that they will want to find out more about Him.

DAY 4 A sick girl and sad lady

KEYPOINT
Faith is **believing** Jesus can help us. He always can, because He is the Son of God.

Today's passages are:
Table Talk: Mark 5v25-34
XTB: Mark 5v21-34

 TABLE TALK

<u>Story One</u>: Jairus's daughter was dying! There was only one person who could help her—**Jesus!** He begged Jesus to come to see her, and Jesus agreed. How do you think Jairus felt as Jesus walked with him towards his house? (*Get ideas.*) But before they got there, Jesus was interrupted! How do you think Jairus felt then? (*Get ideas.*) We have to wait until tomorrow to find out more about Jairus' daughter. How does that make <u>you</u> feel?

 READ

<u>Story Two</u>: On the way to Jairus' house, a lady who was ill came up behind Jesus. **Read Mark 5v25-34**

 TALK

How long had the lady been sick? (v25) (*12 years*) What did she think would happen when she touched Jesus' clothes? (v28) (*She would get better.*) But what did Jesus say was the <u>reason</u> why she got better? (v34) (*She had faith in Jesus.*)

 THINK

It was **Jesus** who healed her—not His clothing! Faith is **believing** that Jesus can help us. He <u>always</u> can! Why? (*Because He is the Son of God, so He is more powerful than any of our problems!*)

 PRAY

"Thank you Lord Jesus that You healed that lady. Help us to believe that You are more powerful than any of our problems."

Building up
Jesus was in a hurry to reach Jairus' daughter, so why do you think He stopped to find out who had touched Him? (*Read v32-34 again. The woman needed to know <u>why</u> she had been healed. It wasn't because Jesus had a special cloak!*)

DAY 5 Don't be afraid—believe

KEYPOINT
Jesus has power over death! It's another powerful sign that Jesus is really God.

Today's passages are:
Table Talk: Mark 5v35-43
XTB: Mark 5v35-43

 TABLE TALK

Recap yesterday's story: What was Jairus worried about? (*His dying daughter.*) Who did he ask to help her? (*Jesus*) But what happened while they were on the way? (*A sick lady touched Jesus' cloak and was healed.*)

 READ

While Jesus was speaking to the healed woman, some men arrived with a terrible message for Jairus. His daughter was dead! **Read Mark 5v35-43**

 TALK

How do you think Jairus felt when he was told his daughter had died? (*Get ideas.*) But what amazing thing did Jesus say to him? (v36) (*"Don't be afraid; just believe."*) What did they hear when they arrived at the house? (v38) (*Crying and wailing.*) The girl had definitely died! But how did Jesus describe her? (v39) (*Sleeping*) What did Jesus do? (v41) (*Took her by the hand and she got up!*)

 THINK

Jesus knew that the girl was dead. He also knew He could bring her back to life as easily as waking her up! Why? (*He has power over sickness and even death—because He is the Son of God.*)

 PRAY

Think of some other wonderful things you know about Jesus, God's Son. (*The earlier stories in Mark will give you some clues.*) Then thank and praise Jesus for being so wonderful!

Building up
Everyone dies, but the coming of Jesus into the world means that death is no longer the end. For those who trust in Jesus, there is the promise of life beyond the grave.
Read John 11v25-26

DAY 6
Home sweet home

KEYPOINT
The people in Nazareth rejected Jesus. They didn't believe that He was God.

Today's passages are:
Table Talk: Mark 6v1-6
XTB: Mark 6v1-6

 TABLE TALK

Play **hangman** to guess the word "Nazareth". Who grew up in Nazareth? (*Jesus*)

READ

Mark has been showing us that Jesus is the **Son of God**. But in today's story Jesus goes home to Nazareth, and meets some people who don't agree!
Read Mark 6v1-6

 TALK

How did the people in Nazareth react at first? (v2) (*They were amazed by His wisdom and power.*) But these people had known Jesus when He was growing up. What did they know about Jesus? (v3) (*He's a carpenter, His mum is Mary, He has four brothers and some sisters.*) They knew Jesus' family, so they <u>didn't believe</u> He could be anyone special! What did they do? (v3) (*They rejected / took offence at Him!*)

 THINK

How sad! These people knew a lot about Jesus, but they ignored the most important things about Him!

PRAY

"Dear God, help us not to ignore the amazing things we read about Jesus. Help us to believe that He really is God. Amen."

Building up
Jesus' miracles are like **signposts** pointing to **who** Jesus is. Look up what John wrote about the miracles in **John 20v30-31**. The people in Nazareth <u>ignored</u> the amazing things Jesus did and said. They <u>refused</u> to believe that He was God. So He didn't do many miracles there (Mark 6v5).

DAY 7
Going fishing!

KEYPOINT
Jesus sent the disciples to tell people about Him. He can use us to tell people, too.

Today's passages are:
Table Talk: Mark 6v7-13
XTB: Mark 6v7-13

TABLE TALK

Make a fishing line by tying a hook (an opened paper clip) or a magnet onto some string/wool. How many things can you catch with your line?

READ

When Jesus called His disciples to follow Him, He said they would be "fishers of men". He didn't mean catching people in a large net! What did He mean? (*Telling people about Jesus.*) In today's reading, Jesus sends the disciples to do some fishing...
Read Mark 6v7-13

TALK

The disciples went out in pairs. What were they to take with them? (*See v8-9*) What <u>didn't</u> they take? (*Money, bread, extra tunic.*) They didn't take money or food. They were to trust **God** for everything.

THINK

The disciples did what Jesus had done—healing people and driving out evil spirits. But it wasn't by their own power! Why were they able to do it? (v7) (*Jesus had given them <u>authority</u> to do it.*)

PRAY

Telling people about Jesus can be really scary. But if you're willing to try, then Jesus will use <u>you</u> as "fishers of men" too! Ask Him to help you.

Building up
The disciples weren't perfect! Did they always <u>trust</u> Jesus? (Check back to Mark 4v38-40!). Did they <u>understand</u> everything about Jesus? (*Not yet, as we'll see later.*) But Jesus still sent them to tell people about Him. Do **you** always <u>trust</u> Jesus? (*Be honest!*) Do you <u>understand</u> everything about Him? (*No?—neither do I!*) But Jesus can still use us to tell people about Him! Thank Him, and ask Him to help you.

DAY 8
Feast for a bad king

KEYPOINT
Herod was very wrong about Jesus. He thought Jesus was John the Baptist come back to life.

Today's passages are:
Table Talk: Mark 6v14-16
XTB: Mark 6v14-29

 TABLE TALK

Think of some reasons for having a feast or banquet. (*E.g. birthday, Christmas, award ceremony...*) In chapter six, Mark tells us about **two kings** and **two feasts**. Tomorrow, we'll read about good **King Jesus**, who gave a feast for thousands. But today's story is about bad **King Herod**, and his drunken feast.

Read the cartoon story in Notes for Parents.

 READ

Later, when Herod heard about Jesus, he was worried... **Read Mark 6v14-16**

 TALK

Who did Herod think Jesus was? (v16) (*John the Baptist.*) But John was dead! So what did Herod think had happened? (v16) (*John had come back to life.*)

Arresting & killing John was <u>very wrong</u>. If Herod thought Jesus was really John come back to life, he was probably <u>very scared</u>. But these weren't Herod's biggest problems. His biggest problem was that he didn't see **who** Jesus really was.

 THINK

Sadly, many people are still very wrong about Jesus today. They think He was just a good man, or that He didn't even exist! They don't understand <u>who</u> Jesus is. Why is that a problem? (*Because believing in Jesus is the only way to have our sins forgiven, and to be friends with God.*)

 PRAY

Think of someone who doesn't understand who Jesus is. Ask God to help them to see the <u>truth</u> about Jesus.

Building up
Read **Acts 4v27-28** to see how God used Herod for <u>His own</u> good purposes. Thank God that no-one and nothing can stop His plans.

DAYS 8 & 9
Notes for Parents

HEROD'S FEAST (DAY 8)
(Based on Mark 6v17-29)

Herod **arrested** John because John told him he was disobeying God (by marrying his brother's wife).

Herod liked to listen to John.

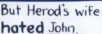

But Herod's wife **hated** John.

Then Herod had a great feast for his birthday.

His wife's daughter danced for him.

Herod liked it, and promised her anything she wanted.

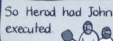

She asked for John to be killed!

So Herod had John executed.

And John's followers buried him in a tomb.

DAY 9
Feast for a good king

KEYPOINT
Nothing is impossible for Jesus our great King!.

Today's passages are:
Table Talk: Mark 6v35-44
XTB: Mark 6v30-44

 TABLE TALK
(*You need bread and fish e.g. tinned tuna.*) Put out five slices of bread and a tin of fish. <u>Ask</u>: If we made fish sandwiches, how many of us could have a filling lunch? Who else could we invite? Could we feed the whole street?

 READ
In today's story, a huge crowd is listening to Jesus. But they're hungry—and there's only a bit of bread and fish to feed them with. **Read Mark 6v35-44**

 DO
(*Optional*) Act the story together.

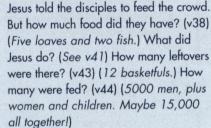 **TALK**
Jesus told the disciples to feed the crowd. But how much food did they have? (v38) (*Five loaves and two fish.*) What did Jesus do? (*See v41*) How many leftovers were there? (v43) (*12 basketfuls.*) How many were fed? (v44) (*5000 men, plus women and children. Maybe 15,000 all together!*)

 THINK
Could you feed your whole street (or school or town) with five slices of bread and a tin of fish? (*No!*) So why could Jesus feed this huge crowd? (*Because He is the Son of God.*)

 PRAY
<u>Nothing</u> is impossible for Jesus! Even the biggest problem is no problem for Him! Ask Him to help you with any problems you are worried about.

Building up
Re-read yesterday's cartoon. In what ways was Herod a bad king? (*He broke God's law by marrying his brother's wife; he made a foolish promise to his wife's daughter; he had John killed as a result.*) Now think about Jesus. In what ways is He a good (perfect!) King? (*Think through previous events in Mark as well as this one.*) Praise and thank King Jesus for being like this.

DAY 10
Water walker

KEYPOINT
Jesus walked on water. Another sign that He is the Son of God.

Today's passages are:
Table Talk: Mark 6v45-52
XTB: Mark 6v45-52

 TABLE TALK
Fill a bowl with water. Ask each person to collect two objects, one that will **float** and one that will **sink**. Put each object on the water to see what happens. What do they think will happen if they <u>stand</u> in the bowl? Will they float on top, or will their feet sink to the bottom? If possible, try it and see! (With a towel ready!)

 READ
The disciples <u>knew</u> that people can't stand on the top of water. That's why they found today's story so terrifying! **Read Mark 6v45-52**

 TALK
The disciples sailed across the sea, while Jesus stayed behind, praying on a hill. How did Jesus get from the hill to the boat? (v47) (*He walked on water!*) Why were the disciples so scared? (v49) (*They thought He was a ghost.*) What did Jesus say to them? (*See v50.*) What happened when Jesus got into the boat? (v51) (*The wind died down.*)

 THINK
<u>We</u> can't stand (or walk) on water—but **Jesus** could! Why? (*He can do all the same things that God can do, because He is the Son of God.*)

 PRAY
In v50, Jesus told the disciples not to be afraid. Think again about **who** Jesus is. Why should that help you not to be afraid? Pray together about your answers.

Building up
Read v46 again. Jesus is God's Son, but it was still important for Him to spend time praying. Do <u>you</u> pray every day? How can you help each other to do so? Pray together now.

DAY 11
Miracle man

KEYPOINT
The miracles show that Jesus is the Son of God, not just a healer.

Today's passages are:
Table Talk: Mark 6v53-56
XTB: Mark 6v53-56

TABLE TALK
In this issue of Table Talk we've read about **six miracles**. List them on six pieces of paper: Jesus stopped a storm; Jesus drove out evil spirits; Jesus healed a sick lady; Jesus brought a girl back to life; Jesus fed a huge crowd; Jesus walked on water. (They happened in this order.)

DO
With younger children, ask them to draw a simple picture next to each miracle. With older children, jumble the pieces up and see if they can put them in the order they happened.

READ
They were amazing miracles! It's not surprising that the news about Jesus spread ahead of Him. People rushed to see Him... **Read Mark 6v53-56**

TALK
What did the people want to touch? (v56) (*Jesus' cloak.*) Does that remind you of one of Jesus' miracles? (*The lady who touched Jesus' cloak and was healed—Day 4.*) But was it Jesus' cloak that healed her? (*No! It was Jesus, not His clothing!*)

THINK
The people who rushed to see Jesus wanted Him to heal them. But the miracles show that Jesus is much more than just a healer. What do they point to? (*He is the Son of God.*)

PRAY
Has reading Mark helped you to understand more about Jesus and who He is? If it has, then thank God.

Building up
Stick your six pieces of paper on the wall. Add one more, with a picture of a signpost, and the words **"Jesus is the Son of God"**.

DAY 12
Fit for God?

KEYPOINT
Keeeping traditional rules does **not** make us "fit for God".

Today's passages are:
Table Talk: Mark 7v5-8
XTB: Mark 7v1-8

TABLE TALK
Imagine that the Queen is coming to visit your house in an hour's time! What would you do to look **fit for the Queen?**

READ
For hundreds of years, the religious leaders had made rules for Jewish people to keep. They believed that keeping these traditional rules made them **fit for God**. One of those rules said you must wash your hands in a special way before eating. If you didn't, you were "unclean" (not fit for God). So, when the religious leaders saw Jesus' disciples eating food without washing their hands in this special way, they challenged Jesus about it.
Read Mark 7v5-8

TALK
Jesus called the religious leaders **hypocrites!** (That means someone who says one thing but does another.) Then He reminded them of the words of an Old Testament prophet (God's messenger.) Which one? (v6) (*Isaiah*) Isaiah said that people honoured God with their words. But what was far away from God? (v6) (*Their hearts.*) The Pharisees kept their own rules. But whose commands did they break? (v8) (*God's*)

PRAY
Do you want to please God? Then do the things He commands. What are some of God's commands? (*If you're stuck, see Mark 12v29-32*). Ask God to help you to obey **Him**, and to make His commands the most important in your life.

Building up
Read v9-13 for an example of how the religious leaders broke God's commands. This was like saying, "Sorry, Mum, no birthday present—I promised it to God instead." They had made their own rules more important that God's!

DAY 13
Heart disease

KEYPOINT
The things that come from the heart are what separate us from God (make us "unclean").

Today's passages are:
Table Talk: Mark 7v14-15
XTB: Mark 7v14-23

DO Think of some of the <u>wrong</u> things you do. Write them in the heart below.

READ The Pharisees worried about what they were like on the **outside**. They thought that breaking their rules (like not washing your hands in a special way) made you "unclean" (<u>not</u> fit for God). But Jesus said it's what you're like **inside** that matters to God. **Read Mark 7v14-15**

TALK What did Jesus say makes us "unclean"? (v15) (*What comes out of us from inside.*)

THINK Look at the things you wrote in the heart. Jesus says that things like these make us "unclean"—not fit for God. That gives us a problem. When our face is dirty, we can wash it. But we <u>can't</u> wash away things like these! Read **Cleaning Up** in **Notes for Parents** to find out how our hearts can be made clean.

PRAY Thank Jesus for dying for you, so that you can be made clean.

Building up
Read Mark 10v45. Thank King Jesus for coming to serve you by dying for you.

DAY 13
Notes for Parents

CLEANING UP
(*A hand mirror may help you think about this.*) If you looked in a mirror, and saw mud on your cheek, what would you do? (*Wash it off.*)

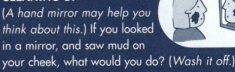

But imagine a mirror that shows what you're like <u>inside</u>. Not your bones and muscles!—but the kind of person you are. What would it show? (*E.g. that you like helping people, or you're good at music, or...*) It would show good things, but it would also show the things you're ashamed of. (*E.g. the things you wrote in the heart opposite.*)

We're <u>all</u> like this inside. We all **sin**. We do what <u>we</u> want instead of what <u>God</u> wants. We'd love to be able to wash these wrong things away—just like the mud—but we **can't**.

Jesus is our Rescuer
But the great news is that Jesus came to <u>rescue</u> us from our sins! When Jesus died on the cross, He took all of our sin onto Himself, taking the punishment we deserve. He died in our place, as our Rescuer, so that we can be forgiven.

Our sin gets in the way between us and God. It stops us from knowing Him and stops us from being His friends. It makes us "unclean"—<u>not</u> fit for God.

But, when Jesus died, He dealt with the problem of sin. That means there is nothing to separate us from God any more. If we have put our trust in Jesus, then we have been forgiven.

Being forgiven is like being washed clean on the inside!

DAY 14
Jesus is...

KEYPOINT
Jesus is the Son of God, the promised King and the only one who can wash our hearts clean.

Today's passages are:
Table Talk: Mark 1v1
XTB: Mark 1v1

 TABLE TALK

(Hide six pieces of paper round the room beforehand. They need to say, "Son of God", "Son of Man", "Friend of Sinners", "Christ", "Messiah", "Saviour".) Ask your child to find the six pieces of paper hidden round the room. They all have names or titles for the same person. Who? (*Jesus*)

 READ

We're nearly half way through Mark's Gospel. (Gospel means "good news".) But today we're going to jump back to the beginning to see what Mark says his book is about. **Read Mark 1v1**

 TALK

What are the two titles Mark gives to Jesus? (*Christ, Son of God*)

Christ isn't Jesus' surname. He wasn't called Mr. Christ! The title *Christ* is a Greek word. (The same title in Hebrew is *Messiah*.) Both titles mean "God's chosen King".

 THINK

The Old Testament is full of promises to the Jewish people saying that God will send them a new King. But that doesn't mean that Jesus only came for <u>Jewish</u> people. The next few stories in Mark's book happened where the **Gentiles** (non-Jews) lived. We're going to see that Jesus came to be King for **everyone**.

 PRAY

Thank God for sending His Son Jesus to be our Rescuing King.

Building up
Write "Jesus is God's chosen King" inside a crown shape. Put it where you will all see it as you continue to read about Jesus in Mark.

DAY 15
Dog food

KEYPOINT
Jesus came for Jews <u>and</u> Gentiles.

Today's passages are:
Table Talk: Mark 7v24-30
XTB: Mark 7v24-30

 TABLE TALK

Think of different ways of dividing yourselves into two groups. (*E.g. male and female, child and adult, love or hate parsnips, can or can't whistle...*)

 READ

The people we're reading about in Mark can be divided into two groups as well: <u>Jews</u> and <u>Gentiles</u> (non-Jews). Jewish people were sometimes called the **children** of Israel. But Gentiles were rudely called **dogs**! Look out for these names in today's reading, where a <u>Gentile</u> woman comes to see Jesus. **Read 7v24-30**

 TALK

What was the woman's problem? (v25) (*Her daughter had an evil spirit.*) Was Jesus able to drive out evil spirits? (*Yes, as we saw on Day 2.*) But Jesus didn't help her straight away. What did He say to her? (*See v27.*)

 THINK

Jesus was the promised <u>Jewish</u> King (the Christ). That's why He said the "children" (Jews) must come first. But the woman wasn't put off! What did she say that "dogs" (Gentiles) get? (v28) (*Crumbs!*) She believed Jesus could help <u>her</u> too. Was she right? (v30) (*Yes! Jesus healed her daughter.*)

 DO

Jesus came for Jews <u>and</u> Gentiles. Add **"Jesus came for EVERYONE"** to yesterday's crown. (*From yesterday's "Building Up" section.*)

 PRAY

Thank God that Jesus came for <u>everyone</u>, including you.

Building up
God had promised Abraham that someone from his family would be God's way of blessing the <u>whole</u> world. **Read Genesis 12v1-3** That person is Jesus!

DAY 16
See hear!

> **KEYPOINT**
> Jesus healed a deaf-mute—just as Isaiah had said that the Christ would do.

Today's passages are:
Table Talk: Mark 7v31-37
XTB: Mark 7v31-37

TABLE TALK: Copy these words from Isaiah onto some paper: "The blind will be able to see, and the deaf will hear. The lame will leap and dance, and those who cannot speak will shout for joy." *Isaiah 35v5-6*

READ: Hundreds of years <u>before</u> Jesus was born, an Old Testament writer called Isaiah wrote these words about the promised King—the **Christ**. They come true in today's story.
Read Mark 7v31-37

TALK: What was wrong with this man? (v32) (*He was deaf and could hardly speak.*) How quickly did Jesus heal him? (35) (*At once.*) How did the crowds feel? (v37) (*Amazed*)

DO: Look again at what Isaiah said. <u>Underline</u> the words that came true when Jesus healed this man.

THINK: Jesus healed this man just as Isaiah said He would. What does that show about Jesus? (*That He's the promised Christ.*)

Read v37 again. The people said, "He has done everything well!" That's true of <u>everything</u> that Jesus has done. Think of some examples. (*E.g. living a perfect life, showing us what God is like, dying as our Rescuer, coming back to life again...*) Use <u>your</u> voices to thank Jesus for these things.

PRAY

Building up
Flick through the headings in Mark looking for evidence that Jesus fulfilled the rest of Isaiah's prophecy (the blind and the lame). <u>Clue:</u> If you can't find them, try Mark 2 and Mark 10.

DAY 17
Action replay

> **KEYPOINT**
> Jesus fed a Gentile crowd, just as He had fed a Jewish crowd. Jesus came for <u>everyone</u>.

Today's passages are:
Table Talk: Mark 8v1-10
XTB: Mark 8v1-10

TABLE TALK: Make a copy of the diagram below. Use it to recap the story of the feeding of the 5000 (Day 9).

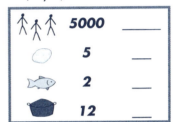

READ: Today's story is very similar to when Jesus fed the 5000, but there are several differences. Listen out for them as you read the story. **Read Mark 8v1-10**

DO: Write in the differences on your diagram. (*4000 men, 7 loaves, a few fish, 7 baskets full of leftovers*).

THINK: There's another BIG difference. The first crowd were mainly <u>Jewish</u>. But this time, there were loads of <u>Gentiles</u> in the crowd. What do you think that shows about Jesus? (*He hadn't just come for <u>Jews</u>—but for <u>everybody</u>.*)

There's another reason why Jesus did the same miracle twice. The clue is in v2. (*Jesus had "compassion for them"—He cared about them.*)

PRAY: Turn these two points into prayers. Thank Jesus that He came for **everyone**—including you. And thank Him that He **cares** for everyone—including you!

Building up
In the Old Testament, God gave food to His people in the desert. **Read Exodus 16v11-18 & 31**. Here Jesus does the same thing. What does that show about Jesus? (*He is the Son of God.*)

DAY 18
Sign language

KEYPOINT
Jesus warns His followers about the teaching of the Pharisees—spreading like yeast..

Today's passages are:
Table Talk: Mark 8v14-21
XTB: Mark 8v11-21

TABLE TALK

Look at some bread. Where do the holes come from? (*Air bubbles as it rises.*) What makes bread rise? (*Yeast*) A <u>tiny</u> bit of yeast spreads through the <u>whole</u> loaf to make it rise. You need to remember that for today's story.

READ

The Pharisees had just demanded a sign from Jesus, but only to test and trap Him. When Jesus got into the boat with the disciples, He <u>warned</u> them about the Pharisees. **Read Mark 8v14-21**

TALK

What did Jesus tell the disciples to watch out for? (v15) (*The yeast of the Pharisees and Herod.*) Jesus is saying that the **teaching** of the Pharisees, who <u>don't</u> believe in Jesus, could spread like yeast. But the disciples miss the point! What do they think Jesus is talking about? (v16) (*Bread!*) To help them understand, Jesus reminds them of two miracles. Which ones? (v19-20) (*Feeding 5000 & 4000.*) The disciples had **seen** these miracles—but missed the point! They haven't seen <u>who</u> Jesus is. (They get it at last in the next two days...)

PRAY

Who do <u>you</u> think Jesus is? Ask God to help you to see Jesus even more clearly as you read the Bible together.

Building up
Read Mark 8v11-13 Miracles are like <u>signposts</u> pointing to who Jesus is. But why are the Pharisees asking for a miracle? (v11) (*To test/trap Jesus.*) Why do you think Jesus refuses to give them a sign? (*He's just fed the 4000! The Pharisees don't want a sign to help them believe—they've already made their minds up about Jesus.*)

DAYS 19-20
Notes for Parents

WHAT DO YOU SEE?
Look carefully at the picture. What can you see?

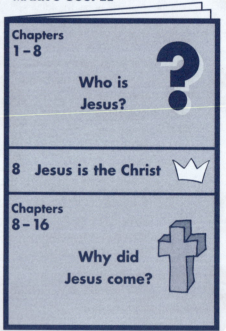

MARK'S GOSPEL

Chapters 1–8
Who is Jesus?

8 Jesus is the Christ

Chapters 8–16
Why did Jesus come?

SEEING CLEARLY
Chapter eight uses "seeing" in two ways: physical sight and spiritual sight. The healing of the blind man is a <u>physical</u> picture of the disciples' lack of <u>spiritual</u> sight. They don't **see** (understand) who Jesus is. And even when they do, they don't understand <u>why</u> Jesus has to die (Mark 8v31-33). They don't yet **see clearly**.

Building up (Day 19)
"Jesus was just a nice man. Nothing else." What could you say to someone who thinks this? Can you use some of the events in Mark's Gospel to explain who Jesus really is?

DAY 19
Seeing in stages

KEYPOINT
We need Jesus' help to be able to clearly see who He is.

Today's passages are:
Table Talk: Mark 8v22-26
XTB: Mark 8v22-26

TABLE TALK

Look carefully at the picture in **Notes for Parents** opposite. What do you see? (*Two faces? Or a vase? Your child may need help to see both.*)

READ

The disciples have **seen** Jesus' miracles, but they haven't **really seen** who Jesus is! Today's story is a picture of that. **Read Mark 8v22-24**

TALK

What was wrong with the man? (v22) (*He was blind.*) What happened when Jesus touched him? (v24) (*He could see, but people looked like walking trees!*) Why is that odd? (*Jesus usually heals people completely and at once.*)

READ

Jesus wasn't having a bad day! He was teaching His disciples something <u>important</u>. **Read Mark 8v25-26**

What happened this time? (v25) (*He could see clearly.*)

THINK

Jesus healed this man in *two* stages to teach His disciples something important. At first the man could <u>not</u> see. Then, he could **see**, but not <u>clearly</u>. Finally, he could **see clearly**. How could that be a picture of the disciples? (*They've seen what Jesus does, but they don't see Him clearly. They don't yet see who He is. And even when they do see who He is [tomorrow!] they still need help to see why He came—which is what the rest of Mark's book is about.*)

PRAY

We need Jesus' help too, if we're going to see Him clearly and get to know Him better. Ask Him to help you.

Building up
See ideas in **Notes for Parents**.

DAY 20
God's chosen King

KEYPOINT
The disciples see <u>who</u> Jesus is at last. He is the Christ (Messiah), God's chosen King.

Today's passages are:
Table Talk: Mark 8v27-30
XTB: Mark 8v27-30

TABLE TALK

Recap from yesterday: What <u>have</u> the disciples seen (i.e. with their own eyes)? (*Jesus' miracles.*) What <u>haven't</u> they seen (i.e. not understood)? (*Who Jesus is.*)

READ

Now at last the disciples eyes are opened. They **see** who Jesus is. **Read Mark 8v27-30**

TALK

Other people had plenty of ideas about Jesus. Who did they think He was? (v28) (*John the Baptist, come back to life. Or Elijah, or one of the other prophets [God's messengers].*) But what did <u>Peter</u> say? (v29) (*You are the Christ/Messiah.*)

What does Christ (or Messiah) mean? (*God's chosen King*) Peter is right! His eyes have been opened at last.

THINK

Look at the diagram of Mark's book in **Notes for Parents**. Today's reading is in the middle section—"Jesus is the Christ". What do you think Mark will tell us next? (<u>Why</u> *Jesus came.*)

Read v30 again. Why does Jesus tell them <u>not</u> to tell people who He is? (*Like the blind man in yesterday's story, they can see who Jesus is, but they don't see clearly. They don't know <u>why</u> He came.*) But we already know the answer! **Why** did Jesus come? (*To die for us, as our Rescuer. Go back to Day 9 if your child isn't sure why Jesus came to die.*)

PRAY

See **Building Up** for prayer ideas.

Building up
Jesus **is** the **Christ**, God's chosen **King**, who came to die as our **Rescuer**. Thank God for sending Jesus, just as He promised. And thank Him for teaching you more about Jesus through Mark's Gospel.

DAYS 21-40
Notes for Parents

THE BOOK OF JOSHUA
Joshua continues the story of the Israelites. It's a story that started in Genesis...

GENESIS
In the book of **Genesis**, God made three amazing promises to Abraham.

1 **LAND** → God promised to give Abraham's family the land of Canaan to live in.

2 **CHILDREN** → God said that Abraham's family would be so HUGE that there would be too many to count!

3 **BLESSING** → God promised that someone from Abraham's family would be God's way of blessing the whole world.

EXODUS, NUMBERS and DEUTERONOMY

700 years later, Abraham's family have become HUGE—just as God promised. They're called the Israelites, and there are over **Two Million** of them!! The book of **Exodus** tells us how they were rescued from Egypt (where they were slaves) and started on their journey to the promised land of Canaan.

God had chosen *Moses* as the leader of the Israelites. In **Numbers** and **Deuteronomy**, Moses led them across the desert to the edge of the promised land. But Moses died there, so the Israelites needed a new leader.

JOSHUA
The new leader of the Israelites is called **Joshua**. God is going to use Joshua to lead the Israelites safely into Canaan.

DAY 21
Get ready!

 KEYPOINT
God is going to keep His promise to give the land of Canaan to the Israelites.

Today's passages are:
Table Talk: Joshua 1v1-5
XTB: Joshua 1v1-5

TABLE TALK
Find out about the Book of Joshua in **Notes for Parents**.

Read the three promises below. What *same* thing does God promise in each?

To Abraham: "I am going to give you and your family all the land that you see." (Genesis 13v15)

To Moses: "I will rescue the Israelites from the Egyptians and bring them out of Egypt to a good and spacious land." (Exodus 3v8)

To Joshua: "Get ready now, you and all the people of Israel, and cross the river Jordan into the land that I am giving them." (Joshua 1v2)

(*Answer: God promises the land.*)

READ
Joshua is the new leader of the Israelites. Read what God tells him about the land. **Read Joshua 1v1-5**

TALK
What are the Israelites to get ready to do? (v2) (*Cross the Jordan river into the land of Canaan.*) What are God's encouraging words in v5? (*Re-read v5*)

PRAY
If you are Christians, then these great words are for **you** too! God will <u>always</u> be with you. He will <u>never</u> let you down! Thank God for being like this.

Building up
Verse 5 is quoted in the book of Hebrews. **Read Hebrews 13v5-6.** Copy the end of Joshua 1v5 onto a large sheet of paper. Stick it somewhere you will all see it—to remind you of God's great promise.

DAY 22
Be strong

KEYPOINT
Joshua is to be strong and brave because God has promised to be with him.

Today's passages are:
Table Talk: Joshua 1v6-9
XTB: Joshua 1v6-9

TABLE TALK

(*Try miming the answers to these questions!*) <u>Adults:</u> When you were children, what job did you want to do? <u>Children:</u> What job would you like to do when you're older? <u>Everyone:</u> Would you want to become the leader of over Two Million people? (Why/why not?)

Joshua has just become the leader of the Israelites. That's a HUGE job! So God gives him some great advice...
Read Joshua 1v6-9

Now read each verse separately, and try to sum it up in your own words. E.g. v6—Be strong and brave; v7—Obey all of my commands; v8—Think about my words all the time; v9—Don't be afraid, I'll be with you wherever you go.

Why do you think Joshua is to be strong and brave? (*Talk about your ideas, then check your answer in verse 9.*)

God has promised to be <u>with</u> Joshua. So Joshua really can be strong and brave! But he also needs to **read** God's Word, **think** about it and **do** what it says (v8). Today, we have much more of God's Word than Joshua did. We have the **whole Bible!** Thank God for the Bible. Ask Him to help <u>you</u> to read, learn and obey it.

Building up
God also encouraged Joshua in a similar way <u>before</u> Moses died.
Read Deuteronomy 31v1-8 & 23. Why do you think God says these words more than once? (*How will it encourage Joshua?*)

DAY 23
Stay or obey?

KEYPOINT
The two and a half tribes kept their promise to help fight for the land of Canaan.

Today's passages are:
Table Talk: Joshua 1v16-17
XTB: Joshua 1v10-18

TABLE TALK

The Israelites are divided into twelve groups, called **tribes**. Two and a half of those tribes had already settled down on the east side of the Jordan river. Look at the map to see which tribes they were.

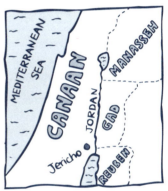

It's now time for the Israelites to cross the Jordan river into Canaan. They will need to fight some battles, so Joshua reminded the two and a half tribes that they had promised to come and fight as well.
Read Joshua 1v16-17

What will they <u>do</u>? (v16) (*Whatever Joshua commands.*) Where will they <u>go</u>? (v16) (*Wherever Joshua sends them.*)

It could have been tempting to stay safely where they were—but they didn't! They promised to obey Joshua and (more importantly!) to **obey God**.

Ask God to help <u>you</u> to obey Him, even when it seems easier not to obey Him.

Building up
Read the whole of **Joshua 1v10-18**. What can the two and a half tribes do <u>after</u> they've helped to fight for the land of Canaan? (v15) (*Return to their own land on the other side of the river.*)

DAY 24
I spy...

KEYPOINT
God used Rahab in His plans.

Today's passages are:
Table Talk: Joshua 2v7
XTB: Joshua 2v1-7

 TABLE TALK

Look again at the map on Day 23. What's the name of the city you can see on the west side of the Jordan? (*Jericho*)

The Israelites are about to cross the Jordan into Canaan. But first, Joshua sends **two spies** across the river to look at the land and check out the nearby city of Jericho. Find out what happened by reading the picture story in **Notes for Parents** opposite.

 READ

With older children read the whole story in **Joshua 2v1-7**. With younger children, just read **Joshua 1v7**.

 TALK

Jericho was a walled city. What happened straight after the king's men left Jericho? (v7) (*The gate was shut.*) The spies were safe for now—but the shut gate means that they were <u>trapped</u> inside the city. Tomorrow we'll find out whether they can escape...

 THINK

Rahab was <u>not</u> one of God's people, yet she helped the spies to hide. **God** used this unlikely person in His plans. Sometimes God uses the most surprising people in His plans. But **He's in control** and always does what's best for His people.

 PRAY

Thank God that His plans always work out for the good of His people.

Building up
God can use <u>anyone</u> in His plans—even His enemies! **Read Acts 4v27-28** for an example of God using Herod and Pilate for <u>His</u> good purposes.

DAY 24
Notes for Parents

Based on Joshua 2v1-7.

DAY 25
Hearing is believing

KEYPOINT
Rahab had heard about God, and believed that He would give Canaan to His people.

Today's passages are:
Table Talk: Joshua 2v8-11
XTB: Joshua 2v8-14

TABLE TALK

Hide <u>seven</u> pieces of paper around the room, with the words *The, Lord, has, given, you, this & land* on them. Ask your child to find the words, and put them into the correct order. <u>Who</u> do they think may have said these words? (*God? Joshua?*)

READ

In fact it was **Rahab** who said this—and she isn't even one of God's people! Use yesterday's cartoon to recap the story, then read the verses to see what else Rahab says. **Read Joshua 2v8-11**

TALK

What had the people in Canaan heard about? (v10) (*How God brought the Israelites across the Red Sea, and how they defeated two enemy kings.*) How did the people feel? (v11) (*They'd lost their courage.*) What did Rahab believe about God? (v11) (*He's the God of heaven and earth.*)

Rahab knew that God would give the city of Jericho to the Israelites. So she asked them to keep her and her family safe. (That's in v12-14.)

PRAY

Rahab knew that God is **God of heaven and earth** (that means God of <u>everything</u>!), that He is **in control**, and that He would **keep all His promises** to the Israelites. Do <u>you</u> believe these three things about God too? If you do, thank Him for each one of them.

Building up
Read Rahab's request for safety in **Joshua 2v12-14**. Rahab was sure that God would give the Israelites victory. Were the two spies also sure? (*Yes!—see their reply v 14.*)

DAY 26
Rahab's rope trick

KEYPOINT
Rahab helped the two spies to escape, and then trusted <u>God</u> to save her.

Today's passages are:
Table Talk: Joshua 2v15-21
XTB: Joshua 2v15-24

TABLE TALK

Use a tape measure or ruler to measure how <u>thick</u> one of your walls is. (This may be easiest in a doorway.) What's the thickest wall you can think of? (*Your garden wall? The wall of your church? My parents live in Chester, where the old Roman walls are thick enough to walk on top of them!*)

READ

The walls of Jericho were so thick that they had <u>houses</u> built into them! That's where **Rahab** lived—in the city wall. Read how the two spies escaped from Jericho. (*If you can, stand by an upstairs window while you read it.*) **Read Joshua 2v15-21**

TALK

How did the spies escape? (v15) (*Down a rope from Rahab's window.*) What did the spies tell Rahab to do? (v18) (*Tie a red cord in her window.*) The spies escaped safely. Later, they went back to Joshua and told him everything that had happened. (v22-24)

DO

The red cord in the window showed that Rahab was <u>trusting</u> God to save her and her family. Hang something red in <u>your</u> window—to remind you that you can always trust God. When you see each other during the day, ask what it means.

PRAY

Thank God that you can always trust Him.

Building up
Read **Joshua 2v22-24**. What were the spies sure about? (v24) (*That God was giving them the land of Canaan.*) They were right!

DAY 27-35
Notes for Parents

THE ARK OF THE COVENANT
(THE COVENANT BOX)

The ark was a wooden box, covered in gold. It was carried on two wooden poles, also covered in gold. Inside the ark were two stone tablets with the Ten Commandments written on them. The ark reminded the Israelites that ***God was with them***.

MAKE THAT BOX!

The ark is very important in the next few chapters of Joshua. Make your own model of it out of a cardboard box. Depending on the size of box, you can use knitting needles, long cardboard tubes or garden canes to act as the carrying poles. You can either punch holes in the box to insert the poles through, or tape them to the bottom edges.

The ark was covered in gold, so colour the box yellow, or cover it with gold paper. If your box opens, you could put a copy of the Ten Commandments (Exodus 20) inside it.

ACT IT OUT

During the next few days we will be discovering exactly how the Israelites were able to cross the Jordan river into Canaan. If you can, **act out** each part of the story together. Make the Jordan by laying two sheets or towels end to end. (*Blue if you have them.*) You can then move one sheet/towel as appropriate to show the water piling up. Ask your children to be the priests holding the model of the ark.

DAY 27
Follow that box!

KEYPOINT
The Israelites had to follow the ark, and trust that God would keep His promises to them.

Today's passages are:
Table Talk: Joshua 3v1-4
XTB: Joshua 3v1-11

TABLE TALK

Play **hangman** to guess the phrase "The Ark of the Covenant".

Ask your child what they know about the ark (sometimes called the Covenant Box), then use **Notes for Parents** to fill in any missing information.

It was time for the Israelites to cross the Jordan river into the land of Canaan.
Read Joshua 3v1-4

READ

What were the Israelites to follow? (v3) (*The ark.*)

TALK

If you read the whole of chapters three and four, you'll find that the ark is mentioned 17 times! It was clearly **very** important! What did it remind the people about? (*That God was with them.*)

DO

Use the ideas in **Notes for Parents** to make a model of the ark. (A model is best, but otherwise make a large picture.) As you make it, talk about <u>why</u> it mattered that God was with the Israelites.

PRAY

The Israelites had to **follow** the ark, and **trust** that God would keep His promises to them. Being a Christian is like that too. We need to **follow** God (by obeying His words in the Bible) and **trust** that He will keep His promises to us. Do you find that hard sometimes? Then ask God to help you.

Building up
Read Joshua 3v5-11. What do these verses tell you about <u>Joshua</u>? (E.g. v7) What do they tell you about <u>God</u>? (E.g. v5, v10)

DAY 28
How to cross a river

KEYPOINT
God stopped the Jordan so that the Israelites could cross. <u>Nothing</u> is too hard for God!

Today's passages are:
Table Talk: Joshua 3v12-17
XTB: Joshua 3v11-17

 TABLE TALK
How many ways can you think of to cross a river? (*Bridge, boat, ford, swim...*)

 READ
To reach the promised land of Canaan, the Israelites have to cross the Jordan river. There are over Two Million of them, including very old people and tiny babies. The river is very wide—and in full flood! There's no bridge, and the people can't swim across a flooded river! Find out how they got across by reading **Joshua 3v12-17**.

 DO
Act this story out, using the suggestions in **Notes for Parents** opposite. As you act it, imagine how the Israelites felt as they crossed the dry river bed.

 TALK
The Ark of the Covenant went first. What did it remind the people? (*That God was with them.*) What is God called in v13? (*The Lord of all the earth.*)

 PRAY
Our God is God of the whole earth! <u>Nothing</u> is too hard for Him! (Not even stopping a flooded river!) That means that God is <u>always</u> able to help you. Pray to Him now about anything you are worried about.

Building up
"Nothing is impossible with God." An angel once said this to a young woman living in Nazareth. Do you know who she was and why the angel came to visit her? Read about it in **Luke 1v35-38**.

DAY 29 Remember remember

KEYPOINT
The Israelites put up a pile of boulders to remind them how God brought them over the Jordan.

Today's passages are:
Table Talk: Joshua 4v1-8
XTB: Joshua 4v1-9

 TABLE TALK
How do you remember things? (*A diary, kitchen calendar, knot in a handkerchief, alarm on your watch...*)

 READ
You probably don't use huge stones! But that's what the Israelites were told to do.
Read Joshua 4v1-8

 DO
Again ***act*** this story out. Remember that the ark was still in the middle of the river bed while the stones were collected. (You could use 12 pebbles, or 12 circular pieces of paper for the boulders.)

 TALK
How many men were chosen, and where were they from? (v2) (*Twelve men, one from each of the twelve tribes.*) What did they do with the boulders? (v8) (*Set them up where they were camped.*)

Imagine, many years later, that a child and parent are walking through the Jordan valley, and they see the stones. The child asks what they mean. What do you think his mum or dad will say? (See v7.)

 THINK
How do <u>you</u> remember the great things God has done for you? (*Talking about them, a Table Talk display, posters or pictures on your walls...*)

 PRAY
Choose some things to remember. (*E.g. God loves you, He sent Jesus to rescue you, He keeps His promises.*) Write them out, and put them where you'll all see them. Then <u>thank</u> God for them.

Building up
Remember some more great things about God by reading **Psalm 100** together.

DAY 30
Flooding back

> **KEYPOINT**
> It was God who stopped the Jordan from flowing, and God who sent it flooding back again.

Today's passages are:
Table Talk: Joshua 4v15-18
XTB: Joshua 4v10-18

TABLE TALK

Recap the story so far, **acting it out** as you go: The people followed the ark to the edge of the river; The priests carrying the ark stepped into the water; At once, the water stopped flowing and piled up, upstream; The people all crossed over on the dry river bed; Twelve men collected huge stones as reminders.

What do you think will happen when the priests with the ark step out of the river bed? Read the passage to find out.
Read Joshua 4v15-18

What happened when the priests left the river bed? (v18) (*The water flooded back.*) If you have used sheets to show the river, move the sheets together again to show the river in flood once more.

Who stopped the water from flowing? (*God*) Who sent the water flooding back again? (*God*) The ark was the <u>first</u> thing into the river bed, and the <u>last</u> to leave it. What did it remind the people about? (*God was with them.*)

If you are Christians, then God is always with **you** as well. Think of some places where He is with you. (*E.g. home, school, work, shopping, with friends...*)
Thank God for this.

Building up
Read **Joshua 3v7** and **4v14**. From that day, the people knew that God was with <u>Joshua</u> too, just as He had been with <u>Moses</u>. Why do you think that mattered? (*E.g. there were scary battles ahead of them.*)

DAY 31
God is great!

> **KEYPOINT**
> Drying up the Red Sea and stopping the Jordan river both show how great God is.

Today's passages are:
Table Talk: Joshua 4v19-24
XTB: Joshua 4v19-24

Recap how the Israelites crossed the river Jordan: God stopped the water; they walked across on dry ground; God send the water flooding back.

Does that remind you of <u>another time</u> when the Israelites needed to cross a lot of water? (*40 years earlier, when God made a dry path across the Red Sea so that the Israelites could escape from the Egyptian army—Exodus 14v21-32.*)

<u>Both</u> of these amazing miracles would show people how **great** God is.
Read Joshua 4v19-24

Where did the Israelites set up the twelve huge stones they had taken from the river bed? (v19) (*Gilgal, near the city of Jericho.*) When children asked what the stones meant, what were their dads to tell them? (v23) (*God dried up the Jordan just as He had dried up the Red Sea.*) What will everyone on earth know? (v24) (*How great God's power is.*)

Joshua told the Israelites that these miracles would show everyone in the world how **great God is**. That includes you (and me!) as we read about these miracles in the Bible. Thank God for showing <u>you</u> how great He is.

Building up
Read about the crossing of the Red Sea in **Exodus 14v21-31**. Compare v31 with Joshua 4v24. What effect did these miracles have on the Israelites? (*They saw God's great power, and honoured Him.*)

DAY 32
Sign of promise

KEYPOINT
The Israelites were circumcised as a sign that they were God's people and ready to trust Him.

Today's passages are:
Table Talk: Joshua 5v1-3
XTB: Joshua 5v1-8

 TABLE TALK

British bank notes have a ***promise*** on them. Have a look at some notes and see if you can spot the promise. ("I promise to pay the bearer..."). You will also find a signature, which is a sign that the bank will keep its promise, and that the note really is worth that amount.

 READ

The Israelites have safely crossed the Jordan river. The local kings have heard how God dried up the river—and they are terrified! So this looks like a great time to start to fight for the land. But there's something the Israelites have to do **first**. Something as a sign of a promise... **Read Joshua 5v1-3**

 TALK

What did God tell Joshua to do? (v2) (*Circumcise the Israelites.*)

Circumcision means having a small piece of skin cut off. It was a **sign** of God's promises to the Israelites, and showed that they were **His people**.

 THINK

When I was at school, my friends and I wanted to show we were Christians. So we made badges to wear saying "God Squad"! It wasn't a very good way to show people what we believed (!!). Can you think of some better ways? (*E.g. by what you **say** or **do**.*)

 PRAY

Ask God to help you to live in a way that shows that you are one of His followers.

Building up
Read Joshua 5v4-8. Forty years ago, the Israelites hadn't trusted God. But now, this new generation are circumcised to show that they are God's people and ready to trust Him.

DAY 33
The promise keeper

KEYPOINT
God always keeps His promises.

Today's passages are:
Table Talk: Joshua 5v9-12
XTB: Joshua 5v9-12

 TABLE TALK

Today's reading links in with three of God's promises. *Copy them onto paper:*
1. God promised to rescue the Israelites from Egypt.
2. God promised to bring the Israelites to the land of Canaan.
3. God promised to look after them (and give them food) on their journey.

 ONE
Read Joshua 5v9

What was the name of the place where the Israelites were? (*Gilgal*) Check the bottom of the page in your Bible to see what Gilgal means. (*To roll/remove.*) God had **rolled away** the shame of living as slaves in someone else's land. Instead, He had given them Canaan to live in. Tick the promise He kept. (*No. 2—to bring them to Canaan.*)

 TWO
Read Joshua 5v10

The Israelites held a special celebration. What was is called? (*Passover*) The Passover meal reminded them how God had **rescued** them from slavery in Egypt. Tick the promise God had kept. (*No. 1—rescuing them from Egypt.*)

 THREE
Read Joshua 5v11-12

What was the special food God had been sending the Israelites? (v12) (*Manna*) God had sent them manna to eat for 40 years! Tick the promise He kept. (*No. 3*)

 PRAY

Thank God that He always keeps His promises.

Building up
Find out more about these promises in **Exodus 3v14-17, 12v1-14** and **16v31-36**.

How to have really HAPPY CHILDREN

Get any group of parents together and ask them a simple question: 'What do you most want for your children?', and you're bound to get back a variety of answers: health, wealth, good friends and safety might all be in the running for the No 1 slot. If you were asking Christian parents, then you would hope that the answer: 'that they should know the Lord' would be up there as well. But boil it all down, and most parents would say that they just want their kids 'to be happy.'

Health, wealth and a good education are what the world assumes will bring our children happiness. And sadly, many Christians buy into the lie that the pursuit of money, comfort and good friendships is what will make our children truly happy, when in reality, it is only to be found in the service of the Living God.

If we want our children to be truly happy, then our aim as parents can never be simply to produce nice, successful people who happen to be Christians. Our aim must be the same aim that Jesus gave the disciples: to make disciples.

How to raise disciples

The fact that you're already reading the Bible with your children using *Table Talk* (or at least attempting to!) is a great start. The Bible informs our minds, and teaches us the truth, but in itself that can be a dangerous thing. Bible knowledge alone will neither save us, nor make us into disciples. We have to help our children to place their trust in God, and to live according to His word. In other words, not head only, but heart and hands as well.

Table Talk gives some suggestions on how to apply the things we learn, but here are some additional suggestions for how we can practically, day by day, teach our children to be disciples in very practical areas of our lives.

Money: Ministers will lament that 'the last part of a person to be converted is his pocket'. And it is true that our habits of thinking and dealing with money are heavily influenced by the world. Make it a priority to make your children treat money and possessions in a Godly way, 'for the love of money is a root of all kinds of evil. Some people, eager for money, have wandered from the faith and pierced themselves with many griefs.' (1Timothy 6v10). This starts with how you talk about it and use it. Do you talk about your wealth as something you have earned, or as a gift from God?

Because children don't know the value of money, and are concrete thinkers, it is often better to have, say, a missionary collecting box in a prominent place at home, or to sign up to a child support scheme, where, for example, you pay for the education of a child in Africa. Giving children pocket money helps them to learn to handle it, and to make choices about giving to the Lord's work. At the same time schemes like Operation Christmas Child in which shoeboxes full of gifts are sent to the poor overseas can also be valuable. For example, when shopping for yourselves with children, you can also buy things to give to others.

Possessions: Children pester constantly with 'I want this, or that.' This is a battle with children that needs to be fought and won again and again. Engaging children with some probing questions can be helpful here. 'Why do you want it?' 'Do you think it will make you happy?' 'What makes you really happy?' This gives you an opportunity to talk about the treasures of Heaven and the wedding feast of the Lamb. It is that that true disciples live for: not the fading joys of this world. *'Sell your possessions and give to the poor. Provide purses for yourselves that will not wear out, a treasure in heaven that will not be exhausted, where no thief comes near and no moth destroys.'* (Luke 12v33). You may have the opportunity to be literally obedient to this command by going to a car-boot sale, or holding a garage sale for some specific project!

Again, the way that you talk about your car, furniture and other prized possessions will set the tone here. We like to look after the things we have, because they are God's gift to us, to be cared for. Try to be thankful to God in prayer for what you have received.

The World: Our instinct as parents is to protect our children from things that will harm or upset them. But we need to start exposing children to the reality of this fallen world, so that they can learn to understand its reality. It is worth occasionally watching the news, talking about it, and praying about it. Following the story of Holly and Jessica, the missing, and then murdered schoolgirls in Soham, Cambridge, was a very significant time for our eldest daughter. It raised lots of questions about danger, and other people, and what our world is like. We prayed for the girls together, and then for the bereaved families. It was distressing for her, but she also understood more of what a world without God is like, and learned to value the good things she had in her family.

And talking honestly about our own weaknesses and failures, and what God thinks of them, is important too. Children tend to think that their parents are wonderful—and then swing full circle when they hit the teenage years. If you are able to talk honestly about your own weaknesses, they are much less likely to become disillusioned with you later on!

This doesn't mean that we will walk around with long faces all the time (remember: those who follow Jesus are truly blessed ones!). But it does mean that we are prepared to be serious and take things seriously.

Friends: perhaps the hardest of all for children to understand. We need to help our children understand that being a follower of Jesus means we are different. We do different things. We find different things important. It may mean that they do not go to see certain films with the rest of their class. It will mean that church always takes a priority over their chosen sport or other activity when it falls on a Sunday. It may mean that they have to 'be a rat' and tell the teacher when something bad has happened. Getting them used to the possibility of this kind of rejection is an invaluable part of their training as followers of Jesus, and will help them to fear God, not man.

> **If we want our children to be truly happy, then our aim as parents can never be simply to produce nice, successful people who happen to be Christians.**

How to be Happy!

Jesus looked at his disciples, and said: "Happy are you poor, the kingdom of God is yours! Happy are you who are hungry now, for you will be filled. Happy are you who weep now; you will laugh! Happy are you when people hate you, reject you, insult you and say that you are evil, all because of the Son of Man!
Luke 6 v 21-22 (GNB)

Do you want your kids to be happy? Then Jesus' way is the only way...

Tim Thornborough

DAY 34
Wrong song

> **KEYPOINT**
> <u>God</u> won the battle of Jericho!
>
> Today's passages are:
> **Table Talk:** Joshua 6v1-5
> **XTB:** Joshua 5v13-6v5

TABLE TALK

Today's story is one of the best known in the Bible. Be ready to act it out, with your children carrying the model ark.

READ

Joshua met a man with a sword (5v13), but this was really **God** speaking to him! God told Joshua what to do. **Read Joshua 6v1-5**

DO

Act out the story: Carry the model ark with you, and have your children pretending to be priests blowing ram's horn trumpets. March around the city (a table?) <u>once</u>, then walk away again. Do this <u>six</u> times in total (as on the first six days). Then march around the table <u>seven</u> times. At the end of the seventh circuit, the "priests" blow one long blast, and everyone gives a shout. Then imagine that the walls have fallen down!

THINK

The **ark** was carried round the walls every time. What did it remind the Israelites about? (*God was with them.*) What was God's fantastic promise in verse 2? (*"I have handed Jericho over to you."*) A popular song in my local schools is, "Joshua won the battle of Jericho". But it's wrong!!! <u>Who</u> won the battle of Jericho? (*God did!*)

PRAY

<u>God</u> was in charge. <u>He</u> gave the instructions. Joshua followed <u>His</u> plans. **Thank God** that His plans always work out.

Building up
Read about the man with the sword in **Joshua 5v13-15**. The ground was **holy** (special to God) because **God** was there, speaking to Joshua.

DAY 35
Wall fall down

> **KEYPOINT**
> The Israelites obeyed God's instructions. So should we!
>
> Today's passages are:
> **Table Talk:** Joshua 6v10-16 & 20
> **XTB:** Joshua 6v6-21

TABLE TALK

Long ago, when armies went into battle, they tried to make as much **noise** as possible, to <u>frighten</u> their enemies. Try ten seconds of mega-noise, to see how much noise **you** can all make by shouting, stamping your feet etc! (*Don't do this if you think it will scare your child.*)

READ

That was the <u>usual</u> way to fight a battle. But the Israelites were told to do things differently... **Read Joshua 6v10-16**

TALK

What did Joshua tell the Israelites? (v10) (*Not to say a word. That means they made no noise at all on the first six days. The only sound was made by the seven priests blowing trumpets.*) When <u>did</u> they make a noise? (v16) (*On the 7th day, after the 7th time round the walls.*) What did Joshua remind the people? (v16) (<u>God</u> had given them the city.)

READ

Read Joshua 6v20

What happened when the people shouted? (*The walls collapsed, and they captured the city.*)

PRAY

God's instructions seemed odd—but the Israelites <u>obeyed</u> Him. Ask God to help **you** to obey Him, even when that's hard or you think that you may be laughed at.

Building up
Try to imagine what this was like for the people in Jericho. Each day they saw the Israelites march round their city and then walk away again! How do you think they felt? And how about Rahab, watching from her window in the city wall? *More about Rahab tomorrow.*

DAY 36
Rescue recipe

KEYPOINT
Rahab <u>trusted</u> God, and she was rescued.

Today's passages are:
Table Talk: Joshua 6v22-25
XTB: Joshua 6v22-27

TABLE TALK Did you hang something red in your window on Day 26? What was it to remind you about? (*The story of Rahab—and that you can always <u>trust</u> God.*)

READ **Recap** the story of Rahab. (The cartoon on Day 24 may help.) After Rahab had helped the spies escape, she tied a red cord in the window. It showed that she was **trusting** God to save her and her family. Read the verses to find out what happened. **Read Joshua 6v22-25**

TALK Was Rahab saved? (v23) (*Yes*) What happened to the city of Jericho? (v24) (*It was burnt.*)

The city was burnt, but Rahab and her whole family were **rescued**. Rahab had been <u>right</u> to trust God!

THINK The New Testament letter of **Hebrews** mentions Rahab. It says she was rescued because of her **faith** (her trust in God). If you have time, read **Hebrews 11v30-31.**

Rahab was right to trust God. His words <u>always</u> come true. How does that make you feel? Talk about it together and then pray about your answers.

PRAY

Building up
Read **Joshua 5v26-27**. Joshua said that anyone who **rebuilt** Jericho would be punished—and that's exactly what happened! 500 years later, a man called Hiel rebuilt Jericho. God kept His promise and punished him. **Read 1 Kings 16v34**. <u>All</u> of God's words come true—the warnings as well as the promises.

DAY 37
Rescue recipe—part 2

KEYPOINT
God sent His Son Jesus to be our Rescuer.

Today's passages are:
Table Talk: John 3v16
XTB: John 3v16

TABLE TALK Talk about different people who might **rescue** us. (*E.g. Fireman if the house is on fire; AA/RAC man if your car breaks down; Lifeboatman if a boat sinks...*)

THINK Yesterday we saw how **Rahab** was **rescued** from Jericho. But in fact the whole Bible is about **God's Great Rescue Plan!** Every person in the world needs to rescued! Do you know what we need to be rescued from? (*Our sin.*)

READ **Sin** is more than just doing wrong things. Sin is doing what **we** want instead of what **God** wants. Sin gets in the way between us and God. That's a HUGE problem, because we <u>all</u> sin. But read about God's great Rescue Plan in **John 3v16**

TALK <u>Why</u> did God send His Son Jesus? (*Because He <u>loves</u> us, and so that we can be <u>rescued</u>.*) <u>Who</u> will be rescued? (*Everyone who believes in Jesus.*)

If you want to know more, check back to **Notes for Parents** on Day 13. Or, for a free booklet called **Why Did Jesus Come?** write to us at: Table Talk, The Good Book Company, 37 Elm Road, New Malden, Surrey, KT3 3HB. Or email me: alison@thegoodbook.co.uk

PRAY Rahab **trusted** God—and God <u>rescued</u> her. If we believe in Jesus, and **trust** Him to save us, then He will <u>rescue</u> us too! Thank God for loving you so much that He sent Jesus to rescue you.

Building up
Find out more about why Jesus came in **Romans 3v22-24**. Thank God for Jesus!

DAY 38
Serious stuff

KEYPOINT
Sin matters. Sin is so serious that God sent Jesus to die for us.

Today's passages are:
Table Talk: Joshua 7v16-23
XTB: Joshua 7v1-26

 TABLE TALK

Note to Parents: This is a very hard passage, but it shows exactly how serious sin is. The just punishment for sin is death. That's why Achan is killed. It is because sin is so <u>serious</u> that God sent His own loved Son to die for us. Use today as an opportunity to thank God for His grace to us, in sending Jesus to take the punishment we deserve.

Read the first part of the story in **Notes for Parents**.

 READ

Find out <u>how</u> God showed them the guilty person in **Joshua 7v16-23**.

TALK

How did God point to the guilty man? (*By choosing his tribe, then clan, then family.*) Who had broken God's rule? (v18) (*Achan*) What had Achan taken? (v21) (*A cloak/robe, some silver and gold.*) What did Achan say? (v20) (*"I have sinned."*)

Achan had **sinned**—he had disobeyed God's command. Achan was killed for his sin. That's how <u>serious</u> sin is.

 THINK

Does dying seem too hard a punishment for Achan? That's because we don't realise how much **sin matters**. Sin is so serious that God sent Jesus to die for us, to take the punishment for our sin.

 PRAY

Ask God to help you to understand how serious sin is. Thank Him for sending Jesus to die in your place.

Building up
Read Romans 6v23 If you have been rescued by Jesus, then **He** has taken the punishment you deserve, and there is no need to fear. If you're not sure whether you've been rescued by Jesus, why not talk to someone from your church, or send for yesterday's free booklet.

DAY 38
Notes for Parents

ACHAN'S SIN
God had said that everything in Jericho was to be **destroyed**, (except for any gold, silver, bronze and iron, which was to be kept in God's treasure rooms). None of the Israelites were to keep anything for <u>themselves</u>. But God's rule was **not** obeyed. So God became very angry with the Israelites...

The Israelites attacked a city called Ai.

They thought God would help them win... ...but He didn't!

Joshua didn't understand what was wrong. So God told him.
Israel has sinned!

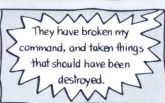
They have broken my command, and taken things that should have been destroyed.

Then God warned them:
I will <u>not</u> be with you unless you destroy those things!

Then God told Joshua that He would show the Israelites exactly **who** the guilty person was.

DAY 39
God's battle plan

KEYPOINT
The Israelites followed God's battle plan to defeat Ai. God's plans <u>always</u> work out.

Today's passages are:
Table Talk: Joshua 8v1-2
XTB: Joshua 8v1-29

 TABLE TALK

(*You will find it helpful to read the whole story beforehand: Joshua 8v1-29.*)

What was the name of the city the Israelites attacked in yesterday's story? Was it Oi? Hi? Ai? or Pi? (*Ai*)

 READ

God had been <u>angry</u> with the Israelites because Achan had stolen things that should have been destroyed. So God <u>didn't</u> help them to capture Ai. But now that Achan has been punished for his sin, God promises to give the Israelites **victory**... **Read Joshua 8v1-2**

 TALK

Who will give victory to the Israelites? (v1) (*God*) How are they to attack the city? (*By ambush from behind.*)

 DO

<u>God</u> made the battle plan. (*It's in v3-9.*) **Act it out** using a table as the city of Ai **or use objects** to show what happened (*e.g. a large tin as Ai, egg-cups to be groups of soldiers*). **This is God's plan:** Joshua chose 30,000 of his best soldiers. They were to hide on the far side of the city of Ai. Then Joshua and his other men would go up to the city. When the men from Ai came out to attack, Joshua and his men would turn and run. The men of Ai would chase after them. Then the hidden soldiers would come out of hiding and capture the city.

It all worked just as God had said! (v10-29) It was <u>God's</u> battle plan, and His plans <u>always</u> work out. Thank God for this.

 PRAY

Building up
Read v2 again. What's the difference this time from when they captured Jericho? (*They may keep the goods and livestock.*)

DAY 40
All all all

KEYPOINT
God's law was read to <u>all</u> the people, including all the children and foreigners.

Today's passages are:
Table Talk: Joshua 8v32-35
XTB: Joshua 8v30-35

 TABLE TALK

God has kept **all** His promises to the Israelites. They're now in the promised land of **Canaan**. And they've defeated **Jericho** and **Ai**. What do you think they will do next? (*Get ideas e.g. have a party, have a rest, attack another city...*)

 READ

Actually, they built an **altar**—a stone table, where they cooked animals as gifts (sacrifices) to God. They made these sacrifices to say thank you and sorry to God. Then Joshua copied something onto stones... **Read Joshua 8v32-35**

 TALK

What did Joshua copy onto stones? (v32) (*God's law, which had been given to Moses.*) The people stood in two groups, facing each other. What was in the middle? (v33) (*The ark.*) What did the ark remind them about? (*God was with them.*) God's words were then read aloud. Who heard them? (v35) (*Everyone—men, women, children and foreigners.*) How much of God's word did Joshua read? (v34) (*All of it.*)

 THINK

God had given the Israelites victory at Jericho and Ai. But the most <u>important</u> things for them to know about wasn't fighting battles! It was about **obeying God's words**.

 PRAY

Thank God for His Word, the Bible. Ask Him to help you to understand it and to obey it.

Building up
Read 2 Timothy 3v16-17 to find out more about God's Word (Scripture). Thank God for each thing that these verses tell us about the Bible.

DAYS 41-55
Notes for Parents

EXPLORING EPHESIANS

Over the next 15 days we are looking at the last half of Paul's letter to the Ephesians. If you have read Issue Five of Table Talk (The Promise Keeper) you may remember these themes:

- What is the focus of Ephesians?—*Unity*
- How?—*Through Jesus on the cross*
- What has He achieved?—*Brought together Jews and Gentiles*
- Why?—*For His praise and glory*

We also looked at some Big words and ideas. *If you have Issue Five available, why not check out the full list on Day 38.*

Spot the Socks!

Paul's letter will show us that being rescued by God should make a <u>difference</u> to the way we live. Our lives should **match** God's rescue. (Like matching socks!)

Can you spare a pair of socks for a couple of weeks? If so, pin labels on them saying "God's rescue" and "Our lives". Put them where you will all see them while reading Ephesians.

MORE TO EXPLORE

We will be looking at the last half of Paul's letter. It builds on all we have learnt from the first half about Jesus on the cross bringing us together in His family.

Paul

The second half is concentrating on how we can live together in Jesus' church, and on what we must do.

It's going to be an exciting and challenging 15 days!

DAY 41
Matchmaking

KEYPOINT
Understanding God's rescue (of us), leads us to live the way God wants.

Today's passages are:
Table Talk: Ephesians 2v5 & 4v1
XTB: Ephesians 2v3-5 & 4v1

TABLE TALK

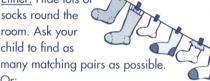

<u>Either:</u> Hide lots of socks round the room. Ask your child to find as many matching pairs as possible.
<u>Or:</u>
Think of some things which go together. (*Table & chairs; knife & fork, bat & ball*). How many can you think of?

READ

Read Ephesians 2v5 (end of verse) and **Ephesians 4v1**

TALK

Can you spot the two things that Paul says go together as a matching pair?

"It is by grace you have been _____"

"I urge you to ____ _ ____ worthy..."

God is calling us to <u>live Jesus' way</u> because of <u>God's rescue</u> of us through Jesus. Find out more next to the matching socks in **Notes for Parents**.

THINK

What words in v1 show that Paul sees this as important? ("*I urge you*") Paul was so excited about what Jesus had done! He wanted everyone to know that God's rescue of people was a free gift because of His love and so we should live <u>His</u> way.

PRAY

Dear God, thank you for your rescue of us through Jesus. Help us to live the way you want.
Amen

Building up
In what ways are <u>you</u> living in God's way? Think of some examples. Ask God to help you.

DAY 42
Notes for Parents

MORE GREAT NEW WORDS
If you used Issue Five of Table Talk (The Promise Keeper) you may remember the new words we learnt on Day 38. Here are some more to help you through the second half of Ephesians.

UNITY
- When a group of people agree about something and work together in friendship.

BODY
- A group of people who believe in God/Jesus/Holy Spirit—the church.

SPIRIT
- The Holy Spirit who lives in believers and enables them to live just like Jesus.

HOPE
- The fantastic future time when we will be with God in heaven for ever.

FAITH
- Believing in God's promises or complete commitment to Jesus.

BAPTISM
- The sign of entering into the church.

APOSTLES
- Someone who has lived with and been taught by Jesus. The eleven disciples, plus Paul, who had been chosen in a special way. Their job —to continue Jesus' work & establish the church.

PROPHETS
- Messengers of God, who spoke on His behalf with a warning or instruction.

EVANGELISTS
- People who tell others about Jesus.

PASTORS
- Those who lead and care for a group of God's people.

TEACHERS
- Those who teach others from the Bible, helping them to understand it.

DAY 42
Stick together

KEYPOINT
Living God's way takes effort and means acting in good ways towards others.

Today's passages are:
Table Talk: Ephesians 4v2-6
XTB: Ephesians 4v2-6

TABLE TALK
What are you like? (E.g. tall, good at football, love chocolate...) Draw a series of pictures to show these things on the top half of a sheet of paper.

READ
Paul wants us to understand all about **unity** and what it means. In our passage a particular number keeps getting repeated. Look out for it as you **read Ephesians 4v2-6**.

TALK
What is the number? (*One*). What does Paul say that there is one of? (v4-6) (*Body, spirit, hope, Lord, faith, baptism and God*). Paul really wants us to understand how important being together and united is. What does he say we need to be in v2? (*Humble [that means not boasting], gentle and patient.*)

THINK
Spend time thinking about how humble, gentle and patient you are. At the bottom of your paper draw three lines, stretching across the page, with *humble, gentle* or *patient* under each line. At the left end of line write 'never' and at right end 'always'. Now put a mark along the line to show where you think you stand for that quality.

How hard does Paul say we must try to stick together? (v3) (*Make every effort/Do your best.*)

PRAY
Think about the qualities you are weak at and ask God to help you to 'make every effort'.

Building up
Look up **Colossians 3v23-24**. What attitude should we have as we live our life for God?

DAY 43
Gifts galore

> **KEYPOINT**
> God has given us gifts so we can work together and achieve amazing things.

Today's passages are:
Table Talk: Ephesians 4v11-13
XTB: Ephesians 4v11-13

DO
Go upstairs and take all your covers off your bed. Now time yourself while you make it alone. How long did it take? Now do it again but with two of you working together. How long did it take? What was the difference?

READ
Today Paul talks about the importance of working <u>together</u> for the same purpose.
Read Ephesians 4v11-13

TALK
What were the different jobs Paul mentions? Check their meanings on Day 42 'More Great New Words'. But this is a small list of gifted people. There are loads more in the church. Can you think of some? Maybe you have some gifts too. What are they?

Why must they be used? (v12)
(*To prepare God's people for works of service.*)

THINK
God wants His church to be united and built up by Christians using their gifts, so they will understand more about Jesus and become more like Him (v13).

How can <u>you</u> use your gifts (the things you're good at) to help other Christians?

PRAY
Dear God, thank you for giving me gifts. Please help me to use them to serve other Christians. Amen.

Building up
Read 1 Corinthians 12v12-20 and see how Paul explains how important we <u>all</u> are in the body of Jesus, the church.

DAY 44
Brand new

> **KEYPOINT**
> Knowing Jesus as our Friend changes how we are. We act differently because we are a new person.

Today's passages are:
Table Talk: Ephesians 4v21-24
XTB: Ephesians 4v20-24

TABLE TALK
When you were a little baby and were taught to walk did you go back to crawling? What other things have you been taught to do which is better than before? (*Ride a bike along; hit a ball with a bat.*) Once we've learnt something amazing we don't want to go back to how things used to be—its not as good!

READ
Read Ephesians 4v21-24

TALK
When we have been taught the truth about Jesus, what should we do with our old way of life? (v22) (*Put off or get rid of it.*) What should we put on? (v24) (*The new self, become new people.*) Who are we like? (v24) (*Created new, to be like God.*)

THINK
We are a Brand New Person because we have heard about Jesus and have been taught the truth (v21). We must get rid of the things we do that don't please God. What things should <u>you</u> get rid of?

PRAY
It is **God** who changes us. Ask Him for help living the new life He's given you.

Building up
Sock sign: The socks are here to remind you that we can't <u>become</u> God's friends by trying to live good lives. It's <u>because</u> God has rescued us that we want to live His way.

Has God rescued **you**? *If you're not sure, check back to Notes for Parents on Day 13.*

DAY 45
Lies are rubbish

KEYPOINT
God has made us new, which means being truthful.

Today's passages are:
Table Talk: Ephesians 2v14-16
XTB: Ephesians 2v14-18

TABLE TALK

How tidy is your room? Is that the truth? When was the last time you had a sort out? It's not only our things which need sorting out, we also need to sort out our lives and get rid of any rubbish.

DO

Draw a mouth in the middle of a piece of paper. Draw faces around it, for specific people you have lied to and write words around it for things you can lie about.

READ

Paul is clear that one thing in our lives, which needs sorting out is...
Read Ephesians 4v25

All the answers to these four questions can be found in verse 25.
- What must we get rid of?
- What must we do?
- Who must we do it to?
- Why?

TALK

THINK

Think of times when you haven't been truthful recently. Why weren't you?

God has made us new to be like Him – and that means being truthful!

DO

Put a big X from corner to corner on your poster and write in big letters 'I AM NEW THROUGH JESUS'.

PRAY

Say sorry to God for not telling the truth. Thank Him for forgiving us because of Jesus. Ask for His help to be truthful and stop telling lies.

Building up
Sometimes telling the truth is a scary thing, but in the Bible we have loads of promises to help us do this. Look up **Deuteronomy 31v6** What is the promise from God to His people?

DAY 46
Temper temper

KEYPOINT
Getting angry is not living God's way—and does a lot of harm.

Today's passages are:
Table Talk: Ephesians 4v26-27
XTB: Ephesians 4v26-27

TABLE TALK

Get off, that's mine!

Get away from me!

Rearrange the letters below to find out what emotion is being shown in these two speech bubbles.

R A N G E

DO

Draw some of your own speech bubbles, showing examples of when you get angry.

READ

Read what Paul has to say about anger.
Read Ephesians 4v26-27

Add three more speech bubbles and write in them the three things the passage says, "do not" do. (Verse 27 means that when we're angry, we give the devil a chance to spoil our friendships with each other and with God.)

THINK

When we get angry it is easy to say nasty things and hurt others, but this is <u>not</u> God's way. What can we do if we do get angry? (Say sorry and mend our friendships. Do it on the same day.)

PRAY

Ask God to help you to obey Him when you feel angry.

Building up
Look up **James 1v19-21** to read some more helpful instructions about dealing with anger. What should we do in v19 and why? (Quick to listen, slow to speak and slow to become angry. It means think carefully before doing or saying things, so that we can be careful what we say.)

DAY 47
Talking rubbish

KEYPOINT
Nasty words hurt and harm, but helpful ones encourage and build up.

Today's passages are:
Table Talk: Ephesians 4v29-30
XTB: Ephesians 4v29-30

TABLE TALK

Look through your clothes and possessions and collect together everything which has a name or logo clearly visible to show where it's from or who made it. (E.g. a Nike tick or three stripes for Adidas; a name on a jumper; or a badge on a football shirt.) What does this show? (*A liking for something or a relationship. A football shirt shows our support or belief in that team.*)

READ

Paul has been helping us to see how we should live to show that we love Jesus. Today's reading does the same.
Read Ephesians 4v29-30

TALK

What needs to come out of our mouths? (*Helpful words to build others up, to make them feel good about themselves.*) Who shouldn't we make sad with our words? (v30) (*The Holy Spirit*)

THINK

When we are rescued by God, He gives us His Holy Spirit so that we can be sure we belong to Him! (That's what v30 means.) What we do and say, with His help, are like a badge or logo to show who we belong to, or believe in.

DO

Think of some kind and helpful things to say to two friends every day this week and DO IT!

PRAY

Ask God to help you to use words to help your friends, not harm them.

Building up
Get the whole family together and sit in a circle. Take it in turns to say two helpful things about the person on your left. Then on your right etc.. Build each other up!

DAY 48
Copycat

KEYPOINT
We must copy Jesus by forgiving others and living a life of love.

Today's passages are:
Table Talk: Ephesians 4v32-5v3
XTB: Ephesians 4v32-5v2

TABLE TALK

Play a guessing game. Think of someone you know (they could be famous) and by acting, or speaking like them, get your partner to guess who it is. Don't say their name. This is called ***imitating***.

READ

Read Ephesians 4v32-5v2

TALK

What three things do we need to do? (v32) (*Be kind, compassionate and forgiving.*) Who should we copy? Who is like this? (v1) (*God*) Who gave up everything for us to forgive and rescue us? (v2) (*Jesus*) What does He make us? (v1) (*Dearly loved children of God.*)

THINK

It is **God** who made us new and we can only change with His help. What can you do to show you are copying God?

PRAY

Thank God for Jesus giving up everything to rescue you. Ask Him to help you to copy Him in the way you treat other people.

Building up
In another of Paul's letters, to the Galatians, he tells us of the fruit of the Spirit. Look up **Galatians 5v22-23** to see what else we should show in our lives. Draw a tree and put each one of these on it as fruit.

DAY 49
Lighten up

> **KEYPOINT**
> Living in the light pleases God—so live in the light.
>
> Today's passages are:
> **Table Talk:** Ephesians 5v8-11
> **XTB:** Ephesians 5v8-11

TABLE TALK: How good are you in the dark? Put a blindfold on and try to find objects you are told to get around the room. Now find the same things with the blindfold off. Which is easier?

READ: When we are in the light, we can see very clearly. That's what it's like being a Christian. **Read Ephesians 5v8-11**

TALK: What did they use to be and what are they now? (v8) (*In darkness—in light.*) What three things show that you are living in the light of Jesus? (v9) (*Being good, righteous (behaving like God) and truthful.*)

THINK: The darkness and light are opposite and don't go together. Living in the light pleases God (v10). Think about the things you do towards others. Do they show that you are a person of the light or dark? How can we find out what pleases God? (*solve the phrase below*)

Read the _ i _ _ e (bbl)

PRAY: You can't be light and dark. Ask God to help you be a light person!

Building up
Get lots of small pieces of paper and a waste paper bin. Write all the following words onto separate pieces of paper. (UNITED, DIVIDED, DON'T PLEASE GOD, GENTLE, HUMBLE, PATIENT, PLEASE GOD, OLD SELF, NEW SELF, ANGER, NASTY, WORDS, LIES, TRUTH, HURTING OTHERS, HELPFUL WORDS, HELPING OTHERS, SIN, KIND, CARING, FORGIVING, LOVING). Now decide which belong to 'light people' and which belong to 'dark people'. Screw up the 'dark people' ones and throw them into the bin.

DAY 50
Be wise

> **KEYPOINT**
> We must be careful how we live and make wise choices.
>
> Today's passages are:
> **Table Talk:** Ephesians 3v20-21
> **XTB:** Ephesians 3v20-21

TABLE TALK: Act out one of the following situations. Say what the <u>choice</u> is and decide what the <u>wise</u> thing to do is.

- Wanting to watch an unsuitable film/video
- Staying at a friends house (your parents don't know them at all)
- Wanting the latest toy craze now

READ: Often, the way we live is all about '**ME**' and no-one else. Paul gives us some very good advice.
Read Ephesians 5v15-17

TALK: What is the warning Paul gives? (v15) (*Be very careful how you live.*) What should we be? (v15) (*Wise*) What should we do? (v16) (*Make the most of every opportunity—that means taking every chance to please God that you get.*) What should we understand? (v17) (*What God's will is.*)

THINK: Being wise is about making good choices, especially in pleasing God. Think about your friends, being at school and at home and talk about choices you have to make to please God. What wise decisions should you make in these three areas?

PRAY: Ask God to help you make wise choices, so that you can please Him.

Building up
Pleasing God in what we do does <u>not</u> save us—but it does show that we belong to Him.
Read Acts 2v42-47 and list some of the things we can do to please God.

DAY 51
Be filled

> **KEYPOINT**
> Be filled and let the Holy Spirit control you, giving thanks to God for everybody.

Today's passages are:
Table Talk: Ephesians 5v18-20
XTB: Ephesians 5v18-20

TABLE TALK What do you do when you are really, really happy? (*Get ideas.*) Lots of people sing or hum or make music. It's a way of celebrating. If you can, sing a song or play some happy music—maybe your favourite Christian song.

READ It's not easy being a Christian and living the way that God wants. But He doesn't expect us to do it alone.
Read Ephesians 5v18-20

TALK What has God given us? (v18) (*His Holy Spirit.*) That means letting Him be in control. What should we always do? (v20) (*Give thanks to God.*)

THINK What does verse 19 say we should do? (*Speak to one another with psalms, hymns and spiritual songs.*) This means we should say kind, helpful and encouraging things to each other. How can *you* do this with those you know? Go and do it!

PRAY Dear God, help me to let your spirit fill me. Help me to sing your praises, always being thankful and encouraging others with kindness and encouragement. Amen

Building up
Sometimes we find it very hard to be so joyful and thankful. We <u>don't</u> go around singing psalms, hymns and spiritual songs. **Read Romans 8v28** to find out how God uses situations, which we struggle with or find hard. (*For our good, even if we don't always understand.*)

DAY 52
Obey OK!

> **KEYPOINT**
> Children must obey parents.

Today's passages are:
Table Talk: Ephesians 6v1-4
XTB: Ephesians 6v1-4

TABLE TALK *Note:* This is an opportunity to be honest with each other. Obeying your parents isn't always easy. Being a parent isn't easy either! Try to be open and honest, and to help each other.

DO Draw a picture of your family. On the left side, write or draw what you <u>like</u> to do with them and on the right side, write or draw what you <u>don't like</u> at home (e.g. going places you have to, not being able to watch things, having to do jobs etc.)

READ Today Paul is writing to families and especially with instructions for children.
Read Ephesians 6v1-3

TALK What are children commanded to do? (v1) (*Obey your parents.*) What does Paul say goes with the commandment? (v2-3) (*A promise that things will go well with you.*)

THINK It's not always easy to obey. Can you think of situations at home when it's hard obeying your parents? Perhaps your picture can help you here. Can you think of times when you have disobeyed? Did you say sorry?

Read Ephesians 6v4
PRAY It's not easy being a parent! Thank God for those who look after you and ask Him to help you to obey them.

Building up
Look up **Exodus 20v1-17** and find out which of the 10 commandments is about children and parents. Cut out a stone tablet shape from card and write this commandment on it.

DAYS 53-54
Notes for Parents

ALL GOD'S ARMOUR
The last chapter of Ephesians includes one of the best known Bible pictures, that of a soldier of God, in full armour. But do we remember all the pieces of armour and their spiritual use.

BELT (v14) *Truth*
- Believe God's word is the truth!
God's truth defeats the lies that the devil tries to get us to believe.

BREASTPLATE (v14)  *Righteousness*
- Believe God loves YOU more than anything!
The devil wants us to believe we are no good and worthless. But God loves us so much that He sent Jesus to die for us. This means He approves of us and thinks we are BRILL!

FOOTWEAR (v15) *Readiness to spread God's Word*
- Tell others about Jesus!
The devil wants us to believe telling others about Jesus is a waste of time. But it's not! We need to be ready to tell others about the fantastic news about Jesus.

SHIELD (v16) *Faith*
- Believe God's promises!
God promises that He will win the battle over the devil. Believing in all God's promises is like a shield for us against doubt and so many other things.

HELMET (v17) *Salvation*
- Believe God has saved you through Jesus!
The devil wants to make us doubt God, Jesus and the promise that we are saved. The helmet protects our minds from doubting God's work of saving us.

SWORD (v17) *God's Word*
- Learn and understand God's Word and use it!
The sword of the Spirit is the only piece of God's armour that is used to attack the devil. It is the Bible, God's word, and we can use it as we trust it.

Why don't you make each piece of armour, out of cardboard, and write the relevant truth about it, on it.

DAY 53
Stand firm

 KEYPOINT
To stand firm against the devil requires us to put on God's full armour.

Today's passages are:
Table Talk: Ephesians 6v10-15
XTB: Ephesians 6v10-15

TABLE TALK

Note: You need cardboard or paper to make armour, and string for the opening game.

Have a game of Sumo wrestling, where you push against each other, to push your opponent out of a small circle. (*Use string to make a circle shape.*) Why did you win/lose?

READ

In a physical battle, our size can be very important. But Paul says that as Christians we are in a different kind of battle.
Read Ephesians 6v10-15

TALK

Who are we battling against? (v11) (*The devil and his schemes.*) What do we have to help us? (v11) (*The full armour of God.*) What are the first three pieces and what do they do? (See **Notes for Parents** opposite.)

DO

As outlined in *Notes for Parents*, make the first three pieces of armour out of cardboard (or draw them on large sheets of paper) and talk about what they are used for, whilst you are making them.

PRAY

When we have God's armour on, the devil can't trick us into believing his lies or disobeying God! That's great news! Thank God for His armour.

Building up
Read Luke 4v1-4, and see what happened when the devil tried to tempt Jesus. Look up **Deuteronomy 8v3**. How did Jesus defeat the devil? (*He used God's Word, the Bible.*)

DAY 54
All God's armour

KEYPOINT
To stand firm against the devil, requires us to put on God's full armour.

Today's passages are:
Table Talk: Ephesians 6v14-17
XTB: Ephesians 6v14-17

What three pieces of God's armour did we learn about yesterday?

Half of the armour is not enough to go into battle! We MUST have the FULL armour of God. **Read Ephesians 6v14-17** and find out what all six pieces are.

The devil's arrows are things like insults, things going wrong and temptations, which we can really struggle with. What does the Shield of Faith do? (v16) (*It puts out the devil's arrows.*) What is the Sword of the Spirit? (v17) (*The Word of God, the Bible.*)

Just like yesterday, make the last three pieces of armour, (out of cardboard or drawn on paper), and talk about what they are used for, whilst making them.

Dear God, please help me to put on ALL your armour. Amen

Building up
Read Luke 4v5-13, and see how the devil continued to tempt Jesus. Look up **Deuteronomy 6v13 & 16**, which were spoken and written down by Moses almost 1500 years before Jesus lived. Jesus used God's Word to defeat the devil. We can too, but what must we do regularly? (*Read and learn God's Word.*)

DAY 55
Keep talking

KEYPOINT
Prayer for ourselves and other Christians, for every situation, is an essential part of living as a Christian.

Today's passages are:
Table Talk: Ephesians 6v18-20
XTB: Ephesians 6v18-20

How do you get to know people? (*By spending time with them and talking to them.*) Make a list of all the Christians you know. (*If you know hundreds, you may have to leave a few out!*) Put the place where they live next to their name.

Paul gives us final instructions to help us live as God's friends.
Read Ephesians 6v18-20

What is the final part of a great Christian life? (*Prayer*). When should we pray? (v18) (*On all occasions.*) Who should we pray for? (v18) (*All the "saints"—which means all Christians.*)

Who does Paul also want the Ephesians to pray for in verse 19? (*Him*) Why? (v19) (*That he will have the courage to tell others about Jesus.*) Who do you know today, who needs this same prayer? (*You could use your list to help you.*)

Pray for those you have thought of, who tell people about Jesus. Pray also for courage for you to tell your friends.

Building up
Read Ephesians 6v19-20 again and go down your list of Christians, putting a mark next to each one who you know teaches the Bible. Pray for them regularly.

DAY 56-65
Notes for Parents

THE BOOK OF JOSHUA
Welcome back to the book of **Joshua**. Last time, we saw how God <u>kept His promise</u> to give the Israelites a **land** of their own—the land of Canaan. He brought them safely across the Jordan river, and defeated the cities of Jericho and Ai.

SETTLING DOWN
The middle of the book of Joshua shows how God helped the Israelites to win many more battles, and then to settle down in the land. (Chapters 9 to 21) *Check out the map below to see where they settled.*

Note: There were over two million Israelites! They were divided into family groups called **tribes**. Each tribe was the family of one of Jacob's twelve sons (Reuben, Simeon, Gad etc). The map shows where each tribe settled down to live.

DAY 56 Always Always Always

> **KEYPOINT**
> God's words are <u>always</u> true.
> He <u>always</u> keeps His promises.
> He can <u>always</u> be trusted.

Today's passages are:
Table Talk: Joshua 21v43-45
XTB: Joshua 21v43-45

TABLE TALK

Read **Notes for Parents** to remind yourselves of the first part of the book of **Joshua**.

READ

We read chapters 1 to 8 of Joshua last time. Now we're going to jump ahead to the end of chapter 21—which sums up everything that's happened so far...
Read Joshua 21v43-45

TALK

How much of the land did God give the Israelites? (v43) (<u>All</u> *that He had promised them.*) How many of their enemies had been able to stand firm against the Israelites? (v44) (*None*) How many of His promises did God keep? (v45) (<u>All</u> *of them.*)

This is the wonderful truth about God:

> God's words are <u>always</u> true.
> God <u>always</u> keeps His promises.
> God can <u>always</u> be trusted.

DO

Copy these sentences onto a large sheet of paper, and decorate it. Put it where you'll see it while reading Table Talk.

PRAY

Look again at these wonderful truths about God. How do they make you **feel**? What do they make you want to **do**? Pray together about your answers.

Building up
One of the great things about reading Old Testament history is that it shows us ***God's character*** so clearly. That's a great thing to share with others, too. Choose someone to write to or visit, and <u>tell them</u> what you have been learning from Joshua. You could give them a copy of the wonderful truths listed above.

DAY 57
Walk in His ways

KEYPOINT
The two and a half tribes were to "walk in God's ways". So are we!

Today's passages are:
Table Talk: Joshua 22v1-5
XTB: Joshua 22v1-5

 TABLE TALK

Look again at yesterday's map. Two and a half of the tribes were living on the East side of the Jordan. Which ones? (*Reuben, Gad and East Manasseh.*)

 READ

These tribes had crossed the Jordan to help the rest of the Israelites to fight for Canaan. (*We read about this on Day 23.*) But now it was time for them to go home... **Read Joshua 22v1-5**

Had the two and a half tribes obeyed God? (v3) (*Yes*) What could they do now? (v4) (*Go back home.*) How were they to live? (v5) (*Obey God's law; love God, serve Him wholeheartedly.*)

 TALK

Some Bibles use the phrase "walk in His ways" in verse 5. This means living your life for God, putting Him first in everything. All Christians are to walk in God's ways. (*That's why this issue of Table Talk is called Footprints.*)

 THINK

Walking in God's ways isn't always easy, but it is always the best way to live. Do **you** want to walk in His ways? (*That means loving God, obeying Him, and serving Him wholeheartedly—just as the two and a half tribes were told to do.*)

PRAY

Ask God to help you to walk in His ways.

Building up
The second half of Ephesians is about walking in God's ways—living in a way that matches His rescue. Look back at the Keypoints for Days 41-55 to remind yourselves of what that means.

DAY 58
Tribal trouble

KEYPOINT
The two and a half tribes didn't want anything in the future to stop them being God's people.

Today's passages are:
Table Talk: Joshua 22v21-27
XTB: Joshua 22v6-34

 TABLE TALK

(*Note:* You will find it helpful to read the full story beforehand: Joshua 22v6-34.)

In today's story, there is trouble between the two and half tribes, and the rest (the other nine and half). Read the cartoon story in **Notes for Parents** to find out how it started.

 READ

The rest of the Israelites were ready to go to war against the two and a half tribes. But first, they sent eleven men to find out why the two and a half tribes had done this... **Read Joshua 22v21-27**

 TALK

The two and a half tribes were horrified! They didn't build the altar so that they could make sacrifices on it. They knew that would be against God's law. Why did they build the altar? (v24) (*They were worried that the river Jordan would divide them from the rest of God's people. Check out the map on Day 56 to see how that could happen.*) What did they want the altar to be? (v27) (*A sign, to show that they were God's people too.*)

 PRAY

The two and a half tribes didn't want anything to happen in future that might stop them being God's people, and living in His ways". Do **you** feel like that too? If so, ask God to help you to keep living for Him all your life.

Building up
Read how the story ended in **Joshua 22v30-34**. What did they call the altar? (v34) (*Witness*)

DAY 58
Notes for Parents

DAY 58—TRIBAL TROUBLE

Based on Joshua 22v6-20.

DAY 59
Joshua's reminder

> **KEYPOINT**
> Joshua reminds the Israelites to be careful to <u>obey</u> God, stay <u>faithful</u> to Him and <u>love</u> Him.

Today's passages are:
Table Talk: Joshua 23v6-11
XTB: Joshua 23v1-11

 Be careful!

TABLE TALK

When might someone warn you to be careful? (*E.g. crossing a road, carrying a precious vase, near a bonfire...*)

 READ

Joshua is now a very old man. It's time for him to tell the Israelites some important things before he dies. He starts by warning them to <u>be careful</u>. Listen out for the words "Be careful" as you read.
Read Joshua 23v6-11

 TALK

What does Joshua tell the Israelites to be careful to do? (v6&11) (*v6—Be careful to obey all God's law; v11—Be careful to love God.*) What else does Joshua tell them to be? (v8) (*Be faithful/hold fast to God, instead of serving the pretend gods [statues] of the people near them.*)

 THINK

Joshua started his speech by reminding the Israelites of all that God had done for them. (That's in v1-5.) Now he says that they should <u>match</u> that (respond to it) by **loving** and **obeying** God, and staying **faithful** to Him.

If you are Christians, then God has done wonderful things for <u>you</u> too. (*He loves you and has sent Jesus as your Rescuer.*) Do you live in a way that <u>matches</u> that? **Say sorry** to God for the times you have let Him down. **Ask Him** to help you to <u>love</u> and <u>obey</u> Him.

 PRAY

Building up
Read the first part of Joshua's speech in **Joshua 23v1-5**. What has God <u>already</u> done? (*Fought the nations for them.*) What <u>will</u> He do? (*Drive out the rest of their enemies too.*)

DAY 60
Joshua's warning

KEYPOINT
We need to protect ourselves from anyone who may try to stop us living for God.

Today's passages are:
Table Talk: Joshua 23v14-16
XTB: Joshua 23v12-16

 TABLE TALK
List some people you know who are from other countries. What do you like best about having friends from other countries?

 READ
Having friends from other countries can be great. But in today's reading, Joshua warns the Israelites <u>not</u> to mix with the other nations around them! Sounds odd? It's because those people prayed to pretend gods (statues) instead of the LORD (the One True God). So Joshua warns the Israelites **not** to start praying to these pretend gods. If they do, there will be a price to pay.
Read Joshua 23v14-16

 TALK
How many promises has God kept? (v14) (*All of them.*) But if the Israelites start to pray to the pretend gods of the other nations, God will be <u>angry</u>. What will He do? (v16) (*He will punish them, so that none of them are left in the land.*)

 THINK
Joshua warned the Israelites not to mix with other nations so they wouldn't start praying to pretend gods. He was *protecting them*. Like the Israelites, we may need to *protect ourselves* from people who try to stop us living for God. (This may mean not spending too much time with them.) See **Building Up** for examples.

 PRAY
Ask God to help you not to be pulled away from Him by anyone (or anything). Thank Him for any Christian friends who help you to live for Him.

Building up
Do you know anyone who makes fun of you for reading the Bible? Or thinks it's silly to believe in Jesus? Or wants you to do wrong things? **Pray** for those people, asking God to help them to change. But you may also need to *protect yourselves* by not spending time with them.

DAY 61
History lesson

KEYPOINT
Joshua reminded the Israelites of their history—and how God kept all His promises to them.

Today's passages are:
Table Talk: Joshua 24v2-13
XTB: Joshua 24v1-13

 TABLE TALK
<u>Either</u>: Play hangman to guess the word **History**, <u>Or</u>: Have a quick search round the house for any books with events from history in them.

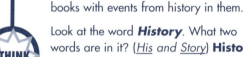

 THINK
Look at the word **History**. What two words are in it? (*His* and *Story*) **History** is **His Story**. It is **God's** story. Today we're listening in on a history lesson, as Joshua reminds the Israelites of their history—and how God kept His promises to them.

 READ
Joshua's history lesson will show that it was **God** who made so many great things happen. As you read the passage, listen out for the word "I" (which means God, because these are God's words.) Every time you hear "I", either stand up, turn around, and sit down again (the noisy version!) or put a tick on a piece of paper (the quiet version!).
Read Joshua 24v2-13

 TALK
Depending on which Bible version you have, you will have heard "I" at least 20 times! <u>Who</u> has been making these great things happen for the Israelites? (*God!*)

 THINK
Now think about **your history** (as individuals or as a family). Think of some things from your own lives that you can thank God for. (Include some people, places or events that have helped you get to know God better.)

PRAY
Now thank God for these things.

Building up
Read another summary of Israelite history (God's story) in **Psalm 136**.

DAY 62
As for me...

> **KEYPOINT**
> Joshua and his family were committed to serving the LORD. Are you?

Today's passages are:
Table Talk: Joshua 24v14-15
XTB: Joshua 24v14-15

TABLE TALK

Imagine working in an old country house as a servant. What might you have to do? Would you like being a servant?

In the next part of Joshua's speech, he talks about **serving** God. But it's not the kind of **servant** you've been thinking about! Or is it...?
Read Joshua 24v14-15

READ

TALK

What did Joshua say that he and his family would do? (v15) (*Serve the Lord.*)

The Bible uses several different ways to describe our relationship with God. It calls us **God's friends**. (John 15v14) It calls us **God's children**. (John 1v12) and it calls us **God's servants or slaves!**

THINK

If we are Christians, then God is <u>in charge</u> of our lives. It's **right** for us to serve Him. And it's also a way of showing our **thanks** to Him.

DO

Jesus said that whenever we serve someone else, we are really serving Jesus! How can <u>you</u> be servants this week? (E.g. weed someone's garden, serve coffee after church, bake a cake for someone who's ill...) Choose something you can do together—then ask God to help you.

PRAY

Building up
Jesus was a servant too! Read what He says about Himself in **Mark 10v45**.

DAY 63 You can't serve God!

> **KEYPOINT**
> Telling God that you will serve Him is easy to **say**, but hard to **do**.

Today's passages are:
Table Talk: Joshua 24v16-21
XTB: Joshua 24v16-27

TABLE TALK

What kind of serving did you decide to do yesterday? Will be easy or hard? Why?

READ

Joshua has just told the Israelites to serve **God** (not the <u>pretend gods</u> of the people around them). But now he tells them something astonishing. He says that they <u>can't</u> do it! **Read Joshua 24v16-21**

TALK

What did the people say at first? (End of v18) (*They will serve God.*) But Joshua needs to be sure they are <u>serious</u> about their decision to serve God. It's an easy thing to **say**—but it won't be easy to **do**. So he warns them about what will happen if they turn away from God. What will happen? (v20) (*God will punish them.*) What did the people say then? (v21) (*They <u>will</u> serve God.*)

The people were <u>serious</u> about serving God. So Joshua set up a large stone as a reminder of what they'd said. (v22-27)

THINK

Joshua's words are true for <u>everyone</u>. We are <u>all</u> sinful. Being sinful means that we want to serve **ourselves** (do what <u>we</u> want) rather than serve **God**. But Jesus came as our Rescuer, to save us from our sins. One of the great things that happens when you are rescued by Jesus is that God starts to <u>change</u> you. One of those changes is that you **want** to serve God.

PRAY

Do <u>you</u> want to serve God? If you do, thank God for making that change in you. But it will still be hard, so ask God to help you to keep wanting to serve Him.

Building up
Have <u>you</u> been rescued by Jesus? If you're not sure, read **Notes for Parents** on Day 13.

DAY 64
Life of a spy

> **KEYPOINT**
> After Joshua died, the Israelites served God until the leaders who'd been with him died too.

Today's passages are:
Table Talk: Joshua 24v29-31
XTB: Joshua 24v28-31

TABLE TALK

Joshua lived a long life, and saw some amazing things. As you read each point below, stop and imagine that *you* had been there too. How would you have **felt**? What would you think about **God**?

- Like Moses, Joshua was born and brought up in **Egypt**.
- He saw the **ten plagues**, and later escaped across the **Red Sea**.
- Joshua was one of **12 spies** sent by Moses to check out the land of Canaan.
- When Moses died, Joshua became the new **leader** of the Israelites.
- God dried up the **Jordan** river so that Joshua could lead the people across.
- Joshua lived to see the Israelites peacefully settled in their new **land**.

Now the time had come for Joshua to die. **Read Joshua 24v29-31**

How old was Joshua when he died? (v29) (*110*) Joshua had encouraged the people to keep serving God. How long did they serve God for? (v31) (*Until the leaders who'd been with Joshua died.*)

Think about what you have learnt about God in the book of Joshua. (*E.g. He always keeps His promises; Nothing is impossible for Him...*)

Praise and thank God for being like this.

Building up
Think back over the life of Joshua. Do you want to be <u>like him</u>? In what ways?

DAY 65
Flashback

> **KEYPOINT**
> God's words always come true.

Today's passages are:
Table Talk: Joshua 24v32-33
XTB: Joshua 24v32-33

TABLE TALK

Flashback One—Joseph

Joseph lived more than 500 years before Joshua. God used Joseph to save his family from famine in Canaan. Instead they went to live in Egypt. When Joseph was very old, he told his brothers what he wanted them to do with his body. **Read Genesis 50v24-26**

READ

Joseph believed that God would <u>keep</u> His promises to take the Israelites back to Canaan. Was he right? (*Yes!*) Read the end of the book of Joshua to find out what happened to Joseph's body.
Read Joshua 24v32-33

TALK

Where was Joseph's body buried? (v32) (*Shechem, in the land of Canaan.*)

Joseph was <u>right</u> to believe God, because God's words always come true. Thank God that His words are <u>always</u> true.

PRAY

Building up
Flashback Two—Abraham
Abraham was Joseph's great grandfather. God made three HUGE promises to Abraham:
Land, **Children** and **Blessing**. (These promises are explained in Notes for Parents on Day 21.)

At the end of the book of Joshua, there are over <u>two million</u> Israelites living in the land of Canaan. Which two promises had God kept? (*Land and Children.*)

God kept His <u>third</u> promise as well. Who did God send as His way of blessing the whole world? (*Jesus—who came as our Rescuer.*)

Thank God for keeping **all** of His promises.

Extra Readings

WHY ARE THERE EXTRA READINGS?

Table Talk and **XTB** both come out every three months. The main Bible reading pages contain material for 65 days. That's enough to use them Monday to Friday for three months.

Many families find that their routine is different at weekends from during the week. Some find that regular Bible reading fits in well on school days, but not at weekends. Others encourage their children to read the Bible for themselves during the week, then explore the Bible together as a family at weekends, when there's more time to do the activities together.

The important thing is to help your children get into the habit of reading the Bible for themselves—and that they see that regular Bible reading is important for **you** as well.

If you **are** able to read the Bible with your children every day, that's great! The extra readings on the next page will augment the main **Table Talk** pages so that you have enough material to cover the full three months.

You could:

- Read **Table Talk** every day for 65 days, then use the extra readings for the rest of the third month.
- Read **Table Talk** on weekdays. Use the extra readings at weekends.
- Use any other combination that works for your family.

WHO IS KING?

These extra readings come from the first four chapters of the book of **Daniel**. In them we meet the powerful king of Babylonia—King Nebuchadnezzar. He needs to learn an important lesson. He isn't really the greatest king at all! He needs to learn that **God** is the real King.

There are 26 Bible readings on the next three pages. Part of each verse has been printed for you—but with a word missing. Fill in the missing words as you read the verses. Then see if you can find them all in the wordsearch.

Note: Some are written backwards—or diagonally!!

K	I	N	G	O	F	H	E	A	V	E	N	S	X	M
N	I	L	O	X	F	I	G	N	W	A	Y	S	T	Y
O	P	N	D	T	U	G	G	Y	I	T	H	A	B	S
W	I	N	G	B	R	H	P	O	D	E	E	R	H	T
L	O	R	D	S	N	O	E	N	E	N	A	G	S	E
E	A	N	I	M	A	L	E	E	O	T	W	I	E	R
D	I	F	F	I	C	U	L	T	T	I	A	S	A	I
G	X	S	K	Y	E	L	S	P	H	M	L	A	S	E
E	T	A	C	S	T	A	T	U	E	E	K	V	O	S
A	B	R	O	W	O	N	D	E	R	S	I	E	N	A
H	E	A	L	T	H	I	E	R	A	I	N	E	S	T
M	N	I	A	T	N	U	O	M	O	D	G	N	I	K

Extra Readings

Chapter 1: Eating veggies!

1 ☐ **Read Daniel 1v1-2**
Nebuchadnezzar thinks he's the greatest king around—but his power really comes from God!
"The L _ _ _ let him capture King Jehoiakim and seize some of the temple treasures."(v2)

2 ☐ **Read Daniel 1v3-7**
Some young Jewish men are to train to serve the king. They include Daniel, and his friends Shadrach, Meshach and Abednego.
"They were to be trained for t _ _ _ _ years." (v5)

3 ☐ **Read Daniel 1v8-10**
Daniel knew it would be wrong to eat the king's food. <u>God</u> made the chief official (Ashpenaz) help Daniel.
"G _ _ made Ashpenaz sympathetic to Daniel." (v9)

4 ☐ **Read Daniel 1v11-16**
Daniel suggested a test. For ten days, he and his friends would just eat vegetables.
"When the time was up, they looked h _ _ _ _ _ _ _ _ _ and stronger than all those who had been eating the royal food." (15)

5 ☐ **Read Daniel 1v17**
God gave Daniel and his friends all the skills they needed.
"God gave the four young men k _ _ _ _ _ _ _ _ _ and skill in literature and learning." (v17)

6 ☐ **Read Daniel 1v18-21**
King Nebuchadnezzar chose Daniel and his friends to serve him—just as God had planned!
"These four knew t _ _ t _ _ _ _ more than any fortune-teller or magician in his whole kingdom." (v20)

Chapter 2: Bad dreams

7 ☐ **Read Daniel 2v1-6**
Nebuchadnezzar had a bad dream. He wanted his advisors to tell him what it meant. But first, they had to tell him what he had dreamt!
"Nebuchadnezzar's dream worried him so much that he couldn't s _ _ _ _ _." (v1)

8 ☐ **Read Daniel 2v7-12**
Nebuchadnezzar's advisors said <u>no-one</u> could tell him what his dream had been.
"What the king asks is too d _ _ _ _ _ _ _ _ _." (v11)

9 ☐ **Read Daniel 2v13-18**
Daniel asked the king for more time. Then he told his friends to pray. He knew that only **God** could help them.
"He told them to pray to the God of heaven for m _ _ _ _ (undeserved kindness)." (v18)

10 ☐ **Read Daniel 2v19-23**
Daniel praised God for showing him the king's dream. He knew that God was the **real King**.
"He controls the times and the s _ _ _ _ _ _ _; He makes and unmakes kings." (v21)

Extra Readings

11 ☐ **Read Daniel 2v24-28**
Daniel told Nebuchadnezzar that only God could explain his dream.
"There is a God in heaven who reveals m _ _ _ _ _ _ _ _ _ ." (v28)

12 ☐
Read Daniel 2v29-35
Daniel described the dream. It was of a huge statue, made of gold, silver, bronze, iron and clay. The statue was then smashed by a rock.
"The rock that struck the statue became a huge m _ _ _ _ _ _ _ and filled the whole earth." (v35)

13 ☐ **Read Daniel 2v36-45**
The dream was about the future. Four great kingdoms would be swept away by <u>God's kingdom</u>, which will last for ever.
"The God of heaven will set up a k _ _ _ _ _ _ that will never be destroyed." (v44)

14 ☐ **Read Daniel 2v46-49**
Nebuchadnezzar had learnt that <u>God is the **real King**</u>.
"Your God is the God of gods and the Lord of k _ _ _ _ and a revealer of mysteries." (v47)

Chapter 3: Fiery furnace!

15 ☐ **Read Daniel 3v1-3**
Nebuchadnezzar built a huge gold statue, and summoned all his officials to come to it.
"King Nebuchadnezzar had a gold statue made, 27 metres (90 feet) h _ _ _ and 3 metres (9 feet) w _ _ _ ." (v1)

16 ☐
Read Daniel 3v4-7
Nebuchadnezzar commanded that <u>everyone</u> must bow down to his statue.
"Anyone who does not bow down and worship will immediately be thrown into a blazing f _ _ _ _ _ _ _ ." (v6)

17 ☐ **Read Daniel 3v8-15**
Daniel's friends (Shadrach, Meshach and Abednego), were near the statue. But they <u>didn't</u> bow down to it!
"They do not worship your gods or bow down to the s _ _ _ _ _ you set up." (v12)

18 ☐ **Read Daniel 3v16-18**
Shadrach, Meshach and Abednego tell Nebuchadnezzar that God is certainly able to rescue them.
"The God we serve is able to s _ _ _ us." (v17)

19 ☐ **Read Daniel 3v19-27**
The three friends were thrown into the blazing furnace. Nebuchadnezzar was amazed at what happened next!
"I see four men w _ _ _ _ _ _ _ around in the fire, untied and unharmed!" (v25)

20 ☐ **Read Daniel 3v28-30**
Nebuchadnezzar was amazed. He had learnt that God really is able to **save** His people.
"No o _ _ _ _ god can save in this way." (v29)

Extra Readings

Chapter 4: Eating grass!

21 ☐ Read Daniel 4v1-3
Nebuchadnezzar wrote Chapter Four himself! He tells us about the amazing things God has done.
"Listen to my account of the
w _ _ _ _ _ _ and miracles the Most High God has shown me." (v2)

22 ☐ Daniel 4v4-14
Nebuchadnezzar had another dream—about a great tree that was cut down, and a messenger from God.
"The tree grew bigger and bigger until it reached the s _ _ and could be seen by everyone in the world." (v11)

23 ☐ Read Daniel 4v15-18
In the dream, God's messenger said that someone would spend seven years living like an animal!
"For seven years he will not have a human mind, but the mind of an
a _ _ _ _ _ _." (v16)

24 ☐ Read Daniel 4v19-27
Daniel told Nebuchadnezzar that _he_ was like the great tree. If he didn't change his ways, he would stop being king and start to live like an animal instead!
"Then you will admit that the Most High God controls all human kingdoms, and that He can give them to a _ _ _ _ _ He chooses." (v25)

25 ☐ Read Daniel 4v28-33
Nebuchadnezzar _didn't_ change. He boasted about how great he was—and suddenly found himself living like an animal!
"He was driven away from people and ate g _ _ _ _ like an ox." (v33)

26 ☐ Read Daniel 4v34-37
After seven years, Nebuchadnezzar's sanity returned, and he became king again. He praised **God** as the _real King_.
"I praise, honour and glorify the
K _ _ _ of h _ _ _ _ _.
Everything He does is right and just."

WHAT NEXT?

We hope that **Table Talk** has helped you get into a regular habit of reading the Bible with your children.

Table Talk comes out every three months. Each issue contains 65 full **Table Talk** outlines, plus 26 days of extra readings. By the time you've used them all, the next issue will be available.

Available from your local Christian bookshop—or call us on **0845 225 0880** to order a copy.

COMING SOON!
Issue Seven of Table Talk

Issue Seven of Table Talk explores the books of Mark, Judges, Ruth and Psalms.
- Investigate who Jesus is and why He came in **Mark's** Gospel.
- Will the Israelites live for God, now that they are settled in the promised land? Find out in **Judges**.
- Meet King David's great grandmother, in the book of **Ruth**.
- Praise and thank God with **Psalms**.